THE FIRST AND SECOND EPISTLES TO TIMOTHY

NEW TESTAMENT FOR SPIRITUAL READING

VOLUME 19

Edited by

John L. McKenzie, S.J.

THE FIRST EPISTLE TO TIMOTHY

THE SECOND EPISTLE TO TIMOTHY

JOSEPH REUSS

CROSSROAD • NEW YORK

1981
The Crossroad Publishing Company
575 Lexington Avenue, New York, NY 10022

Originally published as *Der erste Brief an Timotheus*
and *Der zweite Brief an Timotheus*

from the series *Geistliche Schriftlesung*
edited by Wolfgang Trilling
with Karl Hermann Schelke and Heinz Schürmann

Translated by William Glen-Doepel

Library of Congress Catalog Card Number: 81-68174
ISBN: 0-8245-0128-4

PREFACE

These two letters with the letter to Titus are grouped under the name of "pastoral epistles." They are distinguished from the other letters of the Pauline collection, which are all addressed to churches; these are addressed to individual persons who have official responsibility within churches. They are not yet bishops, but they are the last step we can trace in early Christian literature before the appearance of bishops. The emphasis therefore is on what the church officer should say and do in order that the church members should profess the Christian faith and live the Christian life. This may seem to be a very subtle change from the other Pauline letters, which are addressed to the membership of the churches directly with no reference to the church officers. Yet it is not fanciful to see a step towards the later organization of the church, in which the officers play a much larger role than they play in the New Testament.

Most modern scholars doubt that these letters were written by Paul, or even commissioned by him. It is precisely the difference of structure indicated above which leads to this doubt. The letters are thought to have been written by one or several of Paul's associates, a group which certainly had a hand in the composition of those letters which are called the lètters of Paul without reservation. The attribution of the letters to Paul implies an attitude towards authorship which we in our time and culture cannot share. The letters seem intended to sketch an ideal of church leadership in general and not merely directions for individual officers, and in the mind of their author the letters represented the authentic thinking and teaching of Paul on this topic.

The most distinctly novel interest in the pastoral epistles is the interest in sound doctrine. This has no real parallel in the other Pauline epistles. When Paul talks about the " Judaizers " in the letters to the Galatians and the Corinthians, it is " another gospel " which worries him, not another doctrine; the two words are not synonymous. The doctrine of the early church is not well known to us in content or in structure; in at least some of its uses it signifies the interpretation of the Christ event by the use of texts from the Old Testament. As such the " doctrine " was not the object of faith; it was presented as an explanation of that which was believed. The allusions to the false doctrine of some in the pastoral epistles suggest that the false doctrine included certain speculations about heaven and the spiritual world which are usually associated with Judaism. This type of speculation is found in the apocryphal books of Judaism; in spite of the warnings of Paul, Christians have long shown an interest in this type of speculation.

False doctrine also included the imposition of some observances which the author rejected because they were Jewish observances. Both the speculations and the observances suggest that the false doctrine was a survival of the Judaizing which Paul controverted in earlier epistles. It is interesting that neither in the earlier epistles nor in the pastoral epistles are the false teachers formally expelled from the church. Apparently they were so solidly established in good standing that they could not be formally expelled from the church. And perhaps it did not seem that anyone who differed in doctrine should be formally expelled from the church. That type of crisis called heresy had not yet arisen even at the time when the pastoral epistles were written. The author uses vigorous language of those who teach false doctrine; but in spite of its vigor, he finds room in the same church for himself and his adversaries. One should not mistake this for breadth or tolerance. It would be easier for us to define his attitude if we knew more about the false doctrine which he rejects. He nowhere implies that these false doctrines imply a denial or a doubt of the basic belief that God has saved man in Christ. The supplementing of faith by speculations and observances did not end in the first century, and they have been supported by church officers at least as powerful as the false teachers whom the author of the pastorals controverts.

Certain questions about church discipline arise which are new or at least different from the problems mentioned in the earlier epistles. The passage in 1 Timothy 2:9–15 is not only a faithful echo of 1 Corinthians 14:33–36, it even goes beyond it. Modern interpreters have had some trouble dealing with these passages; it is a recent problem, because up to recent years our culture had departed so far from the ancient world in its attitude towards women that no explanation of New Testament anti-feminism was necessary. Yet it is clear that Paul and his school thought of women as rendering services to the Christian community which men cannot render. The author of First Timothy apparently believes that widows are best equipped for these services; they are old enough to be relieved of family responsibilities and to have acquired wisdom and discretion. The modern reader has to smile at the patronizing attitude of the writer towards young widows. We should like to know more about the services rendered and about the organization in which these services were rendered.

The church of the First Epistle to Timothy had officers called bishops, deacons and elders. The author has told us nothing of the responsibilties and functions of these officers. As we have noticed, the one bishop who rules one church had not yet appeared. The church of the pastoral epistles seems to exhibit a large degree of community responsibility, the type of church order which since the Second Vatican Council is called collegiality. The bishops, deacons and elders each have their own households to rule; they were not professional religious persons, like Paul and presumably the other apostles. We are told nothing of the definition of the " rule " attributed to the elders (1 Timothy 5:17), nor of the care of the church attributed to the bishops (*ibid.* 3:5). A number of allusions scattered through the New Testament indicate that the most organized activity of the apostolic church, if not the only organized activity, was almsgiving. The mandate of almsgiving is abundantly clear in the gospels, but one should not think that it was original with Christianity. It is often praised in the later books of the Old Testament and in the literature of Judaism, and it was practiced generously in Judaism of New Testament times. It is very probable that all the officers mentioned in the pastoral epistles were primarily concerned with almsgiving.

The elders are also concerned with preaching and teaching, but not all of them nor exclusively (1 Timothy 5:17). This is the work of the apostle carried on in the local church by its own officers. These officers would have the responsibility of dealing with the false doctrines with which the letter begins; as we have noticed, no structure yet existed for such problems as this. Who was to judge when doctrine was sound or not? It was only a few years after these letters were written that the church began to manifest a tighter organization in its doctrine and discipline; but this development lies outside the New Testament proper.

JOHN L. MCKENZIE, S.J.

The First Epistle To Timothy

INTRODUCTION

Together with 2 Timothy and the letter to Titus, 1 Timothy belongs to a group known as the " pastoral epistles," which are closely related in form and content. All are addressed to individual persons, even though at the same time they are official documents intended for the churches over which Timothy and Titus presided as pastors. All deal with the duties of the pastoral ministry and contain similar instructions and recommendations. All presuppose the same historical background and have a unity of language, vocabulary, and general tone.

The " pastoral epistles " date from the last period of Paul's life. It is thought that after his release from prison in Rome at the end of his first captivity in the year A.D. 63, Paul went on a missionary journey to Spain, though there is no reliable information about this trip. After that he returned to Greece and Asia Minor, where he visited Ephesus and left his faithful fellow missionary behind him to take his place (1:3; 4:14).

Timothy was the son of a gentile father and a pious Jewish-Christian mother whose name was Eunice (Acts 16:1; 2 Tim. 1:5). He came from Lystra in Lycaonia and was most probably converted by Paul during the latter's first missionary journey (Acts 14:6; 1 Tim. 1:2). While in Lystra on his second journey, the Apostle adopted him as his companion in his missionary labors (Acts 16:1–3), when he was still a young man (4:12). From that moment on he was St. Paul's constant companion almost uninterruptedly.

While in Athens on his second missionary journey, Paul entrusted Timothy with an important mission to Thessalonica (1 Thess. 3:2–6); on his third journey he gave him a difficult commission which brought him from Ephesus through Macedonia to Corinth (1 Cor. 4:17; 16:10f.; Acts 19:22). Timothy accompanied Paul on his return voyage from Corinth to Jerusalem (Acts 20:4) and in his first captivity in Rome (A.D. 61–63) (Phil. 1:1; 2:19; Col. 1:1; Phm. 1). He is mentioned in six different epistles as Paul's fellow worker who is also responsible for delivering the letter (1 and 2 Thess.; 2 Cor.; Col.; Phm.; Phil.). In 1 Timothy, which he wrote probably about A.D. 65 while staying in Macedonia shortly after leaving Ephesus, Paul underlines the tasks which his representative will have to face in that city. These include the struggle against heretics within the Christian community and the preservation of the life and organization of the church.

1. Paul himself had worked as a missionary in Ephesus for three years from A.D. 54–57 (Acts 19). He had now left Timothy there to take his place (1:2) and entrusted him with the task of taking decisive measures against the heretics who were a serious threat to the life of the church (1:18–20; 6:11–16). The information contained in this epistle is not sufficient to enable us to form a clear picture of these heretics, though we know that they were members of the Christian church (1:4; 6:4) and therefore had not completely separated from it. It is clear that they were of Jewish origin, and busied themselves particularly with Jewish fables and genealogies (1:4; 4:7). They boldly claimed to be doctors of the law (1:7), even though they had no idea what the law meant. They prided themselves on their penetrating exposition of sacred scripture and their ardent zeal for the law (see Tit. 1:14). In addition, they prescribed rigorous forms of asceti-

cism which were foreign to Jewish practice, as, for example, the renunciation of marriage (4:3). They also prescribed abstinence from certain types of food (4:3).

These characteristics point to a judaizing doctrine of some kind, such as is known to us also from Colossians 2:16–18. The real reason why these people withdrew from the community and separated themselves from it lay in their rejection of the " sound words " of Jesus Christ and " doctrine which accords with holiness " (6:3). The heretics themselves claimed that their apostasy was based on a deeper insight into the truths of revelation. However, it was really due to their arrogant pride (6:4). Their perverse behavior destroyed the spirit of charity in the church and undermined the fraternal relations of Christians among themselves (6:4f.). St. Paul is particularly severe in his condemnation of the avarice of the heretics which made them regard the practice of their religion as a form of business (6:5).

In contrast to the influence of the heretics, St. Paul points to charity as the goal of Christian proclamation (1:5), and describes the purpose of the old Jewish law in the light of the gospel teaching (1:8–11). To the avarice of the heretics he contrasts the moderation demanded of Christians (6:7f.) and emphasizes the risks run by those who strive for wealth (6:9). The heretics constituted a serious danger to the church at Ephesus and St. Paul, by his apostolic authority, had already excluded two of them, Hymenaeus and Alexander, from the community (1:20).

Notwithstanding the threat they posed to the church, the appearance of these false teachers should not come as a surprise to Timothy or the other members of the community. God's Spirit had foretold it (4:1), and this too formed part of God's plan of salvation. The heretics are nothing less than the instruments of Satan (4:1); they are characterized by their hypocritical piety (4:2) and they bear the stain of sin on their consciences (4:2). Their severe ascetical practices, with their rejection of marriage and abstinence from certain types of food, are contrary to the divine order of creation (4:3f.). Their teachings are " unholy old wives' tales " which Timothy must condemn clearly and without hesitation, and without controversy (4:7; 6:20).

Instead of trying to amass a wealth of possessions, Timothy is exhorted to aim at the virtues which govern his relationship with God and his fellow men (6:11); he must fight the good fight of faith (6:12). In solemn tones, St. Paul calls upon him to safeguard the Christian faith by living a genuinely Christian life, until Christ comes to judge the living and the dead (6:13f.). At the end of his letter, he once more sums up his instructions to Timothy, briefly and concisely; he must preserve faithfully the teachings of the Christian faith, the " deposit which has been entrusted to you," and keep it safe, while emphatically rejecting all false doctrines (6:20).

2. A further task awaiting Timothy at Ephesus was the need to complete the organization of the church. The church had already emerged from the first period of its existence, and the division of office-bearers into " bishops " and deacons was widely established. In this letter Paul lays down the conditions that Timothy must observe and prescribe for admission to the office of " bishops " (3:1–7) or deacons (3:8–13). In Paul's mind, however, these regulations were valid not only for Ephesus, but for the church in Asia Minor as a whole (3:15); this formed part of the universal church, " the pillar and ground of the truth " (3:15). The reason for the demands Paul makes of those who aspire to office is to be found in the sublime glory of " the mystery of piety " which has been entrusted to the church

(3:16). Paul expounds this "mystery of piety" in a sublime hymn to Christ (3:14–16).

Paul also informs his representative of the qualifications necessary for admission to a third type of ministry in the church, the ministry of widows (5:9–16). These women, who were engaged especially in works of charity in the Christian community, must be mature personalities who have proved themselves by a genuinely Christian life (5:9f.). Paul is anxious that younger widows not be admitted to this office (5:11). This attitude was inspired by the dangers which accompanied the work that the widows did in the service of the community (5:11–13). Moreover, he had learned by sad experience that some young widows had already fallen prey to Satan (5:16). It was his wish that these women remarry and perform their duty as mothers (5:14).

3. A third duty facing Timothy was the care of the Christian life of the community at Ephesus. He was responsible for the proper instruction of the community. The teaching of the heretics led to hypercriticism, controversy, and quarreling; in contrast to this, he must never forget that the aim of proper Christian instruction is charity, that genuine vigorous love which comes from a pure heart, a good conscience, and a sincere faith (1:4f.).

Paul is particularly anxious about the care his representative should take in organizing the liturgical worship properly (2:1–15); all mankind, not excluding the civil authorities (2:1–7), must be included in the prayer offered by a Christian community. Such all-embracing prayer is in keeping with the universal salvific will of God; it is God's will that all men be saved (2:4). The prayer offered by a Christian should come from a heart which is pure and free from all anger and dispute (2:8). When they come to pray, women who are Christians should be free from exaggerated care for their appearance; instead, they should be adorned with a God-fearing life and good deeds (2:9f.). Paul forbids women to play a public role in the common liturgical assembly and refers to the duty of motherhood which God has laid upon them (2:12–15). He was probably moved to make this arrangement by abuses in the church. Timothy's relations with the different classes of people and age-groups within the community must be determined by the realization that the community is a family (5:1f.).

It is particularly important and significant that Paul especially recommends the care of the poorest members of the community, of widows (5:3–8) and slaves (6:1f.), to the heart of his representative. He was an experienced pastor and the way he distinguishes between the various classes of widows is striking; he is concerned that the charitable help and support of the community should be directed only to those who were really in need and destitute (5:3, 5). He insists, moreover, on the grave obligation which Christians have towards their parents and grandparents.

Paul was aware of the oppression endured by the numerous slaves in the early Christian churches; they were " under the yoke " (6:1). The directions which he gives his representative in Ephesus refer to slaves who are Christians, whether their masters are pagans (6:1) or Christians (6:2). By their Christian lives and their devotion to duty, they must ensure in every case that " God's name and the Christian teaching is not brought into disgrace " (6:1).

However, the Christian church at Ephesus which was entrusted to Timothy's pastoral care did not consist only of the lower classes of society; there were also wealthy Christians in the community. Consequently, it was his duty to warn these rich Christians of the dangers of wealth (6:17–19). They must put their trust, not in their wealth or possessions, but in God who in his fatherly goodness has care for every one (6:17). They must use their wealth to become rich in good deeds, so that they will be " rich in God's eyes " (Lk. 12:21).

Finally, Paul gives Timothy important instructions concerning the presbyters who presided over the community as a college (5:17, 25). He entrusts him with the duty of arranging for the remuneration of the presbyters who were leaders in the church and busied themselves " with the word and with preaching " (5:17). He also gives the reasons why the church is obliged to provide for the upkeep of these persons (5:18). He is at pains to preserve their reputation from unfounded charges or suspicion (5:19). He gives directions concerning church discipline (5:20) and is anxious to ensure that presbyters who are at fault will be judged impartially (5:21). He is particularly emphatic in reminding Timothy that the selection and ordination of presbyters demands mature consideration and serious investigation (5:22, 24f.), if he is to avoid incurring the guilt for the sins of others (5:22).

The more exemplary the life of its pastor, the more flourishing will be the life of the community. Despite his lack of years (4:12), therefore, Timothy is bound to show himself an " outstanding servant of Jesus Christ " in the whole conduct of his life; the " word of the faith " and the " wholesome doctrine " of Christianity must be his rule of life (4:6, 12). Instead of observing the rigorous asceticism of the heretics, he must devote himself to living in accordance with that piety which carries with it the promise of eternal life as a saving gift (4:8). Moreover, he must be careful of his weak health (5:23). Until Paul returns, he should devote himself to " reading, exhorting, and teaching" (4:13). At the time of his appointment to office he received a special gift of grace from God for all his duties; he must not neglect this. His fidelity to Christian teaching and his exemplary life will bring both him and his community to eternal salvation (4:15f.).

OUTLINE

The Opening of the Letter (1 : 1–2)

INTRODUCTORY VERSES (1 : 1–2)

I. The sender and the addressee (1 : 1–2a)

II. Greetings (1 : 2b)

The Body of the Letter (1 : 3—6 : 19)

THE STRUGGLE AGAINST HERESY: TIMOTHY'S SPECIAL TASK IN EPHESUS (1 : 3–20)

I. A description of the heretics (1 : 3–7)

II. The purpose of the law in the light of the gospel (1 : 8–11)

III. Paul's gratitude for being chosen to proclaim the gospel (1 : 12–17)

IV. Renewed appeal for the struggle against heresy (1 : 18–20)

THE ORGANIZATION OF THE CHURCH (2 : 1—3 : 16)

I. The conduct of liturgical worship (2 : 1–15)

1. Prayer for all men, especially those in high positions (2 : 1–7)
2. Rules of behavior for men and women in the liturgical assembly (2 : 8–15)

II. Office-bearers (3 : 1–13)

1. The qualifications of "bishops" (3 : 1–7)
2. The qualifications of deacons (3 : 8–13)

III. The reason for these regulations: the sublimity of the divine mystery which is entrusted to the church (3 : 14–16)

THE HERETICS AND THEIR INNOVATIONS (4:1–11)

I. The prohibition of marriage and certain foods (4:1–5)
II. Correct Christian practice (4:6–11)

INSTRUCTIONS TO TIMOTHY CONCERNING HIS OFFICE (4:12—6:2)

I. An exhortation to lead an exemplary life and be zealous (4:12–16)
II. Correct treatment of the various age-groups (5:1–2)
III. Widows (5:3–16)
   1. The care of widows (5:3–8)
   2. The office of widows (5:9–16)
IV. Presbyters (5:17–25)
V. Slaves (6:1–2)

FURTHER REFERENCES TO THE HERETICS (6:3–19)

I. The pride and greed of the heretics (6:3–10)
II. An appeal to Timothy to fight the good fight (6:11–16)
III. The correct use of wealth (6:17–19)

The Close of the Letter (6:20–21)

CONCLUSION (6:20–21)

I. A final warning against heretics (6:20–21a)
II. Good wishes (6:21b)

THE OPENING OF THE LETTER
(1:1-2)

INTRODUCTORY VERSES (1:1–2)

The Sender and the Addressee (1:1–2a)

[1]*Paul, an apostle of Jesus Christ, commissioned by God our saviour and Christ Jesus our hope,* [2a]*to Timothy, his own son in the faith.*

Our letter is addressed to Timothy who had been Paul's fellow worker and his disciple for years. Yet Paul lays great stress on the dignity of his office as an apostle; he is an "*apostle*," an authorized ambassador of Jesus Christ, and he adds that he is "commissioned by God." What is the point of this reference to his authority, to the commission he had received? The epistle is not merely a private letter addressed only to Timothy; it is an official document, a communication from the Apostle. It is intended primarily, of course, for Timothy, but it is also addressed to the whole church at Ephesus. Behind Timothy stands the Apostle of the gentiles with the fullness of his authority; behind Paul stands Christ himself and God. It is from God that the message comes to the community; therefore the Christians are bound to be doubly attentive.

In this letter Paul means to strengthen the position of his fellow missionary and deputy in the community. He is anxious to give him the support he will need in all the problems concerning the struggle against heresy, the organization of the church, and the various difficulties in the life of the community. Hence the need, not merely for attention, but for obedience to the message the letter brings. This comes from " God our saviour " and redeemer, through Paul. The redemption of the human race and its salvation is rooted ultimately in God himself. " It was God's good pleasure to bring those who have faith to salvation by means of the folly of our preaching " (1 Cor. 1:21). As a result of the redemption, Christians have become a " new creature " (2 Cor. 5:17); all this they owe to " God who has reconciled us to himself through Christ " (2 Cor. 5:18). It is by " grace " that we are " saved; it is God's gift " (Eph. 2:8).

Paul writes here as one who has been " commissioned by Jesus Christ our hope." Jesus Christ is the hope of Christians for this life and above all for the next. It is he who accomplished our salvation on the cross and thereby merited every grace for the human race; his redemptive act is the cause and the basis of the salvation of all mankind. Without Christ, Christians would have " no hope " (1 Thess. 4:13), just like pagans.

The letter is addressed to Timothy, " his own son in the faith." Timothy was the son of a pagan father and a pious Jewish-Christian mother. It seems probable that he was converted to Christianity by Paul in Lystra on his first missionary journey. That is why Paul calls him his " beloved and true son in the Lord " (1 Cor. 4:17); he shares the sentiments of his spiritual father, Paul. In the Epistle to the Philippians, Paul praises him with the words, " I have no one who shares my mind as he does; he is genuinely concerned with your affairs . . . You know how he has proved his loyalty; he took part with me in serving the gospel, like a son helping his father " (Phil. 2:20–22). How like the Apostle his disciple must have been: this son must truly have resembled his father; he must have been united to him in the closest fidelity and love, that Paul could say such wonderful things about him.

Greetings (1 : 2b)

2b*Grace, mercy, and peace, from God the Father and Christ Jesus our Lord.*

Instead of the usual Greek or Jewish greeting (" Joy," " Peace "), Paul wishes his correspondent *grace, mercy, and peace.* He raises the normal greeting in use at the time to a Christian level and wishes him all that seems most important in his eyes: " grace," the inexhaustible wealth of divine favor, which man can only receive, but never merit by his own efforts; " mercy," which is so necessary for sinful man, when we remember his complete dependence upon God and the distance between them; " peace," which we might better translate as " salvation." It includes man's eternal destiny, as well as everything else. Only God and Jesus Christ could be the source of such gifts. As God's Son and the risen Lord, Jesus is his equal and stands on the same level with him. This greeting is not meant to be an idle wish; it is intended to be effective, so that Timothy and the community will really receive the fullness of grace, mercy, and salvation. The fact that God is our " Father " and Jesus Christ is " our Lord " ensures this.

THE BODY OF THE LETTER
(1:3—6:19)

THE STRUGGLE AGAINST HERESY: TIMOTHY'S SPECIAL TASK IN EPHESUS (1:3–20)

Most of Paul's epistles can be divided into two parts. First he recalls all that God has done and expounds his saving activity. In the second part he then draws various conclusions from this concerning the Christian life. The First Epistle to Timothy, however, follows a different and looser pattern. Paul's instructions for the struggle against heresy and the different problems concerning the organization and life of the church are set down at random, one after another.

In this letter Paul wants to encourage Timothy to take firm and decisive steps in the struggle against the heretics who were making their appearance in Ephesus. At the same time, he wishes to bolster his position as head of the church and that of his representative, by giving him the support of his word as an apostle. In the opening chapter of his letter, therefore, he describes those heretics who were propagating Jewish legends and had set themselves up as teachers of the law (1:3–7). As it happened, their conception of the law was completely false, as is clear from the gospel (1:8–11). The mention of the gospel with which he had been entrusted moves Paul to make a public protestation of gratitude to God for choosing him to proclaim the good news (1:12–17). In this context he once more calls upon Timothy to fight against the adulteration of the gospel message by the heretics (1:18–20).

A Description of the Heretics (1:3–7)

3 *On my departure for Macedonia I asked you to stay in Ephesus,*

to make it clear to certain people that they must not preach false doctrines . . .

After his first imprisonment at Rome (A.D. 61–63), Paul went on a missionary journey of which we have no record. On this occasion he left Timothy behind him at Ephesus as head of the local Christian church and his own representative, while he continued his journey into Macedonia. He had worked as a missionary in Ephesus himself for three years from A.D. 54–57 (Acts 19). On the return voyage to Jerusalem, he said good-bye to the elders of the church in Ephesus at Miletus. There he warned them especially to be watchful (Acts 20:31). He had taken the opportunity to tell them in advance that after his departure, "People will come from your own ranks, teaching a perverse doctrine, to win disciples who will follow them" (Acts 20:30). As he was leaving Ephesus, he had already ordered Timothy to take firm measures against "certain people," that is, the heretics. He reminds him of this in this letter and at the same time gives him the support of an official document coming from an apostle, in his dealings with the community.

It was no longer possible for Paul to remain in person in all his earlier missionary foundations; he could no longer exercise vigilance over the Christian churches unaided. That is why he appointed his disciples and fellow workers as his representatives and installed them as heads of the churches. Timothy was now indispensable at Ephesus, so that he could no longer accompany Paul on his missionary journeys. The prophecy that Paul made when he said good-bye to the elders at Miletus had now been fulfilled. People had risen up in the church who talked perversely.

These heretics were still members of the Christian church, yet they constituted a grave danger. They had strayed into paths of error and now posed a serious threat to the community as a whole. The tares which the enemy had sown among the wheat had now appeared. All through the course of history, the church will have reason to repeat to herself the warning which the Lord gave long ago to his disciples in the parable of the tares and the wheat (Mt. 13:24–30). Wherever the Lord sows clean seed in his field, the enemy will come and sow his tares among the wheat. When the seed grows and bears fruit, the tares will also appear.

4. . . *or occupy themselves with legends and interminable genealogies which give rise to disputes rather than contribute to God's salutary training in the faith.*

What kind of doctrine did the heretics teach in Ephesus? Paul gives us no further information. He says only that they busied themselves with "legends and interminable genealogies." We can be sure in any case that he is referring to rabbinical legends which were devoid of truth and of any foundation in reality. It is most likely that these included far-fetched stories and assumptions concerning the Old Testament genealogies. With their unimaginably long lines of descent, these were bound to produce a deep impression. These erroneous doctrines clearly imply Jewish origin. At the same time, they show traces of a later and very dangerous heresy, gnosticism.

More important than a closer description of this heresy, with which Timothy was familiar in any case, were the effects which were visible in the community. These false doctrines inspired controversy, quarrels, and disputes about unimportant matters. They contributed nothing towards that training in God's salvation which is based on the true and unadulterated teaching of the faith. Any doctrine which is contrary to revealed truth as it is proclaimed by the church in her teaching office will always lead to the same evil results. In one way or another, it will destroy the spirit of charity and peace in the community. It is incapable of contributing to that training in salvation which God offers us in the faith; its whole purpose is frustrated.

5The goal of our instructions is the love which comes from a pure heart, a good conscience, and a sincere faith. 6Certain people have strayed from this path and turned to empty chattering.

In contrast to these heretical teachings, Paul now underlines the goal of proper Christian instruction and the correct teaching of the faith. This goal is *love,* love of God and of one's fellow men. To be genuine and effective, however, this love presupposes three things. It must spring from a " pure," clean heart which is free of all self-interest or evil desire; from a " good conscience " which is assured of its union with God in all its thoughts and actions; and from " a sincere faith " which is free from all pretense. Such a faith is based on genuine conviction, not on an ostentatious display of theological speculation, as was the case with the heretics.

The heretics ignored the whole purpose of Christian instruction and preaching. They neglected the three requirements which are necessary for genuine Christian love. Therefore, their teaching was reduced to " empty chattering." They say a lot but miss the whole point of the Christian message. For all their explanations which seem so profound, they are like " echoing brass or a clanging cymbal " (1 Cor. 13:1). Their preaching is an empty chattering.

Paul's condemnation of the heretics' teaching is severe. If the instruction which is given in the Christian church is not directed towards its real ultimate goal, true and genuine love, it always degenerates into a vain series of empty propositions.

7They want to act as teachers of the law; yet they do not know what they are saying, nor that about which they are so assured.

Paul has a further reproach to make against these heretics. They boldly claim to be " teachers of the law "; yet they are not clear about the meaning of the law themselves. They claim a knowledge of the Old Testament law and its significance for the New Testament community of salvation which they do not possess. They are anxious to be praised for the subtlety of their scriptural interpretations, and also for their zeal for the law and the harsh ascetical practices (4:3) which they impose on the community. Their whole attitude tended to replace faith with worthless human science, and love with observance of the law. It showed that they had failed to understand both the gospel and the Old Testament. In Paul's eyes, their teaching was merely " empty chatter." The Apostle now feels compelled to give a brief description of the role and the real purpose of the Old Testament law, to counteract their false doctrine.

The Purpose of the Law in the Light of the Gospel (1:8–11)

In earlier letters Paul had gone deeply into the relationship between the Old Testament law and Christian teaching. This is true, for example, of the Epistle to the Galatians, which was a polemical document; and of the Epistle to the Romans, which gave a broader and calmer presentation of the problem. In perfect harmony with these writings, Paul now outlines the proper Christian viewpoint concerning the old law, in a few short strokes.

8 *We know that the law is good, if a person applies it as the law intends,*
9 *namely, in the realization that it is not intended for the just man, but for the lawless and insubordinate, for godless people and sinners, for the unholy and the profane, for those who kill their father or mother or their fellow men,*
10 *for the impure and those who sin against nature, for kidnappers, liars, perjurers, and all those who indulge in any activity contrary to sound doctrine . . .*

In this sentence Paul includes himself with all other Christians and asserts first of all that *the law is good.* Why? Because it comes from God, the Lord of all, and has a divinely appointed purpose to fulfill. This is to prepare the way for the Christian economy of salvation. It is the " tutor who brings us to Christ " (Gal. 3:24). With Christ, however, " the purpose of the law " has been achieved (Rom. 10:4). The law is good now only " if a person applies it as the law intends "—that is, if it is applied in a manner in keeping with its own internal purpose. It must not be invoked where it does not apply, if it is to be reconciled with the spirit of the gospel.

For a " just man " there is no longer any exterior law imposed from without. Such a person has been converted from a life of sin by God's grace; he is separated from the sinful world. God has called him and granted him the fullness of new life in Christ. Anyone who has been freed from sin by Christ is exempt from the law; he lives now by *faith* and not by the law. A Christian makes his own the real purpose of the law; his whole life, his entire personality is molded by it. For him the law has lost its character as a penal code.

The law still has force as a means of discipline, as a norm imposed from without, for those who are still subject to sin, for the " lawless," as Paul calls them in the catalog of vices which now follows. All these vices are opposed to the teaching of the gospel which he describes as the " sound doctrine." This teaching is the perfect expression of spiritual and moral health and it promotes a sound and morally irreproachable life. Anything which contradicts the teaching of the gospel is sick; it contains the germ of disease and leads to a dissolute life. The law also has force for those who allow themselves to be guided by such unwholesome doctrine.

By adopting this attitude towards the old law, Paul leaves far behind the viewpoint of those who insisted on its literal observance. Instead, he arrives at the idea of Christian freedom. The freedom of the children of God leaves all purely exterior conformism far behind. Christians have been rescued from sin and refashioned by the grace of Christ. They must now mold the conduct of their lives in virtue of the new principle of life they have received. The dignity of the Christian which Paul proclaims is certainly exalted. The Christian who follows the sound teaching of the gospel has been justified by Christ. He must now allow his conduct to be determined by God's gift of love which dwells in him. This has become his " law," to the exclusion of all else.

[11]. . . *according to the gospel of the glory of the blessed God I have been entrusted with.*

The proclamation of this freedom from the old law is part of the teaching of the gospel entrusted to Paul. This gospel brings us a revelation of that divine glory which is proper to the last stage of time. In his eternity and immortality, God enjoys the highest degree of blessedness. With justifiable pride and emphasis, Paul adds that he personally was chosen by God to make known this gospel and have it committed to his care. The vivid realization of his unworthiness in the sight of God is matched only by the strength of his conviction that he was chosen by God. His heart overflows with gratitude as he recalls all that God's grace has accomplished in him and through him. " By God's grace I am what I am " (1 Cor. 15:10).

Paul's Gratitude for Being Chosen to Proclaim the Gospel (1:12–17)

12*I give thanks to him who has given me strength, to Christ Jesus our Lord; he decided I was worthy of trust and took me into his service . . .*

In his polemic against the heretics, Paul cites his apostolic authority and the fact that he had been entrusted with the gospel. This reminds him of the day of grace he experienced at Damascus. He owed his vocation as an apostle exclusively to the compassionate kindness of his Lord Jesus Christ. It is inconceivable and almost a miracle in his eyes that the Lord should have taken him into his service, that he should have *decided he was trustworthy* and shown confidence in him. In 1 Corinthians Paul himself insists that the " servant of Christ and steward of God's mysteries " must " show himself worthy of trust " (1 Cor. 4:2). Christ had decided that he was worthy of such trust and he gave him the strength to justify this confidence. It is for this incredible proof of the merciful love of his Lord that Paul gives thanks. His heart overflows with gratitude and he constantly reminds Christians that they must be grateful to God. Indeed, the great difference between Christians and pagans is that Christians are always and everywhere giving thanks to God, so that such " expressions of gratitude are multiplied beyond measure and give glory to God " (2 Cor. 4:15).

13 *. . . although I had formerly been a blasphemer, a persecutor, and a criminal. Yet I found mercy because I had acted in ignorance and disbelief.*

To emphasize the wonder of God's mercy, Paul draws a sharp contrast between his life in former times and now. These were the two great periods in his life, the years before his conversion at Damascus and those which followed it. In his earlier days he had been a " blasphemer "; he reviled the name of Christ and all that he had done, and persecuted his church with unrestrained hatred and violence. In his speech before Agrippa he himself describes how he vented his rage on Christians: " I threw many of the saints into prison . . . When they were put to death, I gave my voice for it. I tried many times, in synagogues all over the country, to torture them into blaspheming. There was no limit to my rage against them and I even persecuted them in foreign cities " (Acts 26:10f.). He confesses, " I persecuted God's church without restraint and tried to destroy it " (Gal. 1:13).

Paul refers again and again to the hatred he once felt for Christ, his teaching and his followers. How could God have chosen him as his apostle, despite all that? For this miracle of grace there is only one explanation in Paul's eyes, *"I found mercy.*" In God he found that incomprehensible mercy and love of which he, " a blasphemer, a persecutor, and a criminal," was totally unworthy. In his " ignorance and disbelief " Paul had failed completely to grasp the mystery of Christ. However, this did not diminish his guilt; it merely explained how such mercy on God's part was possible at all. The inconceivable, forgiving, and merciful love of Christ who said on the cross, " Father, forgive them. They do not know what they are doing," extended even to him (Lk. 23:34).

14*The grace of the Lord revealed itself in overflowing measure with faith and love in Christ Jesus.*

When Paul looks back over his life before his conversion at Damascus, he can only offer thanks to God. Again and again he gives thanks for the incredible mercy which was shown him. There could be no doubt that he had experienced the incomprehensible riches of God's mercy and grace " in overflowing measure." However, God's graciousness extends even further. Together with his mercy, he bestowed on Paul that *faith* and *love* which have their source in Jesus Christ and are centered on him. As a result of his conversion, Paul enjoys new life, the life which comes from being united with Christ. It is this which enables him to have faith in his Lord and to love his brothers. In this way, God's infinite and incomprehensible mercy is constantly at work in him.

15*This saying is worthy of credence and fullest approval: Christ Jesus came into the world to save sinners, among whom I am the first.*

Paul takes up the same idea once more and sums up all that he has said in a well-known formula of Jewish origin. It is probable that the expression he chooses was part of a profession of faith which was familiar to Christians and was frequently used by them; " Christ Jesus came into the world *to save sinners*." As the fullness of time dawned, Jesus Christ, the only-begotten Son of God who was with the Father from all eternity as his Son, came into this world. The purpose of his coming was the salvation of sinners, the redemption of mankind. Mankind had gone astray and been separated from God by sin, so that it incurred God's anger. Jesus himself told the chief publican, Zaccheus, " The Son of man has come to seek out and to save what was lost " (Lk. 19:10).

In his own conversion, Paul himself had personally experienced the reason why Jesus Christ became man—to save sinners. His own conversion together with God's calling and choice of him was one instance of the saving activity of Jesus Christ which is the redemption of sinners. He had been one of those who were lost and had incurred God's just anger. Indeed, he was one of the worst; he was " *the first among them*." Of course, his guilt has now been blotted out, but it remains a constant motive of humility and gratitude for him. He is conscious of his absolute dependence on the all-holy God and his infinite mercy. It was this which had called him and made him an apostle, despite his hatred of Christ and the fact that he persecuted his disciples. That is why he refers to himself as " the least of the apostles, not worthy even to be called an apostle, because I persecuted God's church " (1 Cor. 15:9). He is " the least of all the saints " (Eph. 3:8). Paul had experienced the excess of God's grace. The more deeply he penetrated God's infinite love and compassion, the more he grew in humility in God's sight and the more fervent was his gratitude.

16 *The reason I found mercy was that Jesus Christ might show in me first of all the extent of his forbearance, as an example for those who would believe in him, to gain eternal life.*

Paul now comes to his last and most important point; he acknowledges the reasons God had for showing him such mercy. In God's plan of salvation, there was a special reason for his conversion and the vocation he received. As he had been the first among sinners, so now he must be first among those who received the gift of grace. In Paul, Jesus Christ demonstrated the fullness of his mercy and compassion, so that he became an *example* for all those to whom God would later show mercy. In him the whole world could see how those who put their faith in Christ and build their lives on him as on a foundation stone can attain salvation and eternal life. His conversion and God's choice of him were to be a model for the mercy God would later show to others, and so reveal the infinite forbearance of Jesus Christ. Like him, others too can and should rise from the depths of sin and error by God's merciful love and so win faith and salvation. Paul's case is irrefutable evidence that no one is so lost from God's sight that Christ's infinite mercy and unfathomable love cannot reach him. Christ came " to seek out and to save those who were lost " (Lk. 19:10).

17 *To the king of ages, the immortal, invisible, and only God belong honor and glory for ever and ever. Amen.*

This outburst of praise is perfectly natural in a prayer of thanksgiving. The thought that God chose him and the revelation of God's goodness this involved almost force Paul to his knees, *to praise God.* He finds a suitable formula in the text of a liturgical prayer which must have been often used in the common worship of the Christian community. It later found a place in the canonical hours of the church (at prime). The " King of Ages " has a right to such adoration. It is he who makes the ages follow one another until Christ comes again and all the ages reach their completion. He is exalted far above all ages and all creation; in the midst of change he remains the same and his years know no end. He is the " immortal God," the source of life and the giver of all life. He is the " invisible God " who dwells in the abyss of light, whom no human being can see. He is the " only God," completely superior to all creatures. It is to this God who has shown such merciful love in the redemption of sinners that honor and glory belong for ever. It is hard to imagine how we could adore God or praise him more worthily at the beginning of each day than with these words which have been adapted from our epistle and form part of the divine office.

Renewed Appeal for the Struggle Against Heresy (1:18–20)

After this brief glance back at his own conversion (1:12–17), Paul returns once more to the point at issue. He makes a fresh appeal to his disciple and representative to fight against the adulteration of the gospel by the heretics.

[18a]*I want to impress this strongly upon you, Timothy my son, in accordance with the predictions which were made to you before . . .*

Paul addresses Timothy personally, calling him " my son." Paul had been instrumental in giving Timothy eternal life by converting him to the Christian faith and Timothy shared the same sentiments as his spiritual father. In virtue of this close relationship, Paul now calls upon him to proclaim the gospel and the teaching of Christ as he has expounded it in the preceding verses (1:3–11). At the same time, he reminds Timothy of *prophecies* made some time previously which concerned him, about which we of course know nothing. In any case, they foretold that Timothy would have a great influence in preserving the truth of the gospel. What are we to think of these prophecies? It is most likely that they involved some extraordinary manifestation of the Spirit, some message or prediction referring to Timothy made under the influence of the Holy Spirit, by people who had the gift of prophecy. This may have happened when Paul was looking for a deputy before leaving Ephesus. We know of a similar occurrence in Paul's own life; together with Barnabas, he was chosen for the work of the apostolate at the instigation of the Holy Spirit, which was made known by a prophet.

Paul, therefore, was not moved by purely human motives, when he appointed the youthful Timothy as his representative in Ephesus; he chose him at the instigation of the Holy Spirit. *God's Spirit* watched over the churches and pointed out those who should be entrusted with the difficult task of succeeding the Apostle of the gentiles. That was the way it was in Ephesus in the first century, and that is the way it always is in the church, although God's will is not always made known explicitly by prophecy. Our Lord himself promised his disciples, "Behold, I am with you all days until the end of the world" (Mt. 28:20).

[18b]*. . . so that you may fight the good fight on the strength of them* [19a]*with faith and a good conscience.*

The prophecy concerning Timothy should give him strength to bear his responsibilities in Ephesus and "fight the good fight," especially the fight against the misinterpretation of the gospel. Paul likes to compare the Christian life and especially the life and ministry of those who bear office in the church to the life of a soldier. As the soldier of Jesus Christ, he who bears office must be similarly equipped for the struggle and for suffering. That is why Paul calls upon Timothy as a good soldier of Christ, chosen by the words of a prophet, to "fight the good fight."

The most important piece of equipment he has for this struggle is *faith* and *a good conscience*. Faith and a good conscience go together; they give him the strength to overcome error. Anyone who enters this struggle with a weak or wavering faith, or with a conscience which is sullied or stained with sin, is bound to go under. In the struggle for the gospel, Timothy must stand firm in the faith; in everything he does he must allow himself to be guided by the voice of a good conscience, that is, by God's own voice. The Christian life is like a military campaign undertaken for God; that is why it demands a constant struggle. The man who is determined to win must have a firm faith and a pure and good conscience.

[19b]*Some have rejected this and made shipwreck of the faith.* [20]*Among them are Hymenaeus and Alexander, whom I have given over to Satan, to be corrected, so that they will not blaspheme.*

The serious nature of the struggle is illustrated by the fate of certain persons of whom Paul mentions two by name, as a frightening example for others. How did their downfall begin? They "rejected a good conscience." They rejected as a tiresome burden the moral obligations which their consciences prescribed. Their ruin began with an unrestrained and immoral way of life. They became the plaything of their own passions and consequently could not avoid "making shipwreck of the faith." The way which Paul refers to is one which has often led Christians from moral weakness, lack of self-control, and enslavement to passion, to final apostasy from the faith.

Hymenaeus and Alexander were probably fellow workers of Paul and Timothy in Ephesus. In any case, they were known to Timothy. Paul says that he has "given both of them over to Satan," probably on his departure from Ephesus; their lives and their doctrine constituted a danger which threatened to destroy the whole community. We have no detailed information how they were handed over to Satan. They were probably dealt with in the same way as the person guilty of incest at Corinth, whom Paul also made over to Satan (1 Cor. 5:5). Presumably the two heretics were excluded from the community of the faithful and also from participating in the celebration of the Eucharist. This should serve to "correct" them and bring them to their senses, until they were finally able to return to the community.

Such exclusion from the church at Ephesus was a question of church discipline. It was done for the good of the community, not from personal motives. Otherwise, the spiritual life of the community would have been destroyed. It was also for the good of the sinners themselves; they were prevented from multiplying their sins. Those who were excommunicated were not excluded from the church definitively by being "handed over to Satan." This severe penalty was intended to make them *amend their lives,* if they submitted to it. Paul compares himself to a mother nursing her child to whom she has given all the love of her heart (1 Thess. 2:7f.). He feels anxiety for the church entrusted to him and suffers like a mother in childbirth for the Christians for whom he was responsible (Gal. 4:19). Yet he was also aware that he enjoyed Christ's authority and had power to "bind and loose." His successors in the church, the bishops, are bound to exercise the same pastoral love and also the same pastoral authority.

THE ORGANIZATION OF THE CHURCH (2:1—3:16)

In the second part of his letter, Paul gives his disciple and representative important instructions concerning the community life of the church, and first of all for the proper regulation of divine worship (2:1–15). He is anxious that the prayers offered by Christians should include all men and the civil authorities in particular (2:1–7). He is especially worried about the proper behavior both of men and women in the liturgical assembly and at prayer (2:8–15). The appointment of office-bearers is vitally important for the community (3:1–13), and Timothy is reminded of the qualifications necessary for "bishops" (3:1–7) and deacons (3:8–13). The reason for these prescriptions is explained in a hymn to Christ by referring to the sublime dignity of the mystery entrusted to the church (3:14–16).

The Conduct of Liturgical Worship (2:1–15)

Prayer for All Men, Especially Those in High Positions (2:1–7)

[1]I recommend, in the first place, that prayer, entreaty, intercession, and thanksgiving, should be offered for all men, [2]for kings and all those in authority, so that we may live a calm and peaceful life in all dutifulness and decency.

Care for the proper regulation of the liturgical assembly takes first place among the instructions that Paul sends to his representative. We know that at the beginning the liturgical worship of the primitive church imitated the practice of the Jewish synagogue very closely and adopted its precisely regulated forms. We also know, however, that in the areas evangelized by Paul the charismatic influence of Christians who were endowed with the gifts of the Spirit, speaking with tongues and prophecy, was allowed greater scope for development. Various abuses which Paul tried to abolish, together with the decrease in numbers of those who enjoyed such gifts, led to the need for closer organization. As Paul himself said, " God is not a God of disorder, but of peace " (1 Cor. 13:33).

Christians used to come together in the common assembly where they found themselves united in a spirit of brotherly communion, to listen to the word of God and celebrate the Eucharist. Paul now asks that they should offer public prayers in common as the deepest expression of a fervent Christian community life. Most probably these prayers followed on the reading and explanation of sacred scripture. The four different terms Paul uses for prayer—" prayer, entreaty, intercession, thanksgiving "—are not intended to be a complete enumeration of all the different types of prayer. They are merely an all-around description of Christian prayer. They mean that prayers of all types should be offered.

This common prayer—and this is the point that Paul emphasizes—must include *all* mankind without exception or limitation. A Christian's charity extends to all men and knows no limit or restriction; similarly, his prayer must include the entire human race. He must omit no one, much less exclude anyone. God's fatherly goodness embraces all men; " he makes his sun rise upon the good and the bad, and the rain fall on the just and unjust " (Mt. 5:45). In the same way, a Christian must pray for all men, if he wants to show himself a child of his Father who is in heaven.

One group of persons for whom public prayer should be offered is mentioned in particular. These are "*kings,*" that is, the Roman emperors—at that time, Nero—and "*those in authority.*" These were the senior Roman officials and especially the governors of the different provinces. Besides the obligation of obedience to the authorities appointed by God, there is an obligation of prayer. This obligation holds good for all time, quite independently of the religious affiliation of those who wield temporal power.

Christians should see the reason for such prayer in their need to live "a calm and peaceful life." They must realize, indeed, that God thinks so highly of the Christian church and loves it so much that he will take its welfare into account in determining the course of history. They know that God's blessing and protection will ensure the expansion of Christianity.

Another point which is clear from these directions is the relationship between the Christian community and the *authority of the state.* Pagans adored the emperor as a god, while the Jews prayed for his material well-being; Christians, on the other hand, must pray because it is God's wish. This obligation of prayer, which binds the whole community, does not depend on the situation in which Christians or the authorities find themselves, no matter what it may be. This recommendation to pray remains in force even in the case of a godless regime. God's will to bring all men to salvation continues to be valid in their case too, as Paul goes on to explain immediately.

[3]*This is good and pleasing in the sight of God, our saviour,* [4]*who wants all men to be saved and attain knowledge of the truth.*

Paul states emphatically that such all-embracing prayer for the entire human race, including the civil authorities, is "*pleasing*" to God. He is our "saviour," the redeemer who wants "all men to be saved" from his anger. In Paul's eyes, this is the ultimate reason for the obligation to pray for all men, God's universal salvific will. It is his wish that all men should be saved, that they should be rescued from sin, death, and judgment, and brought to "knowledge of the truth" of his revelation; they must be brought to conversion and finally to salvation. God's love and God's saving will know no bounds, no limits. In the same way, the prayer offered by the Christian community must know no bounds or restrictions.

5*For there is only one God and one mediator between God and*
men, the man Christ Jesus 6*who gave himself up as ransom for*
all men, a testimony borne at the appropriate time.

God's universal salvific will is now set forth in three different phrases with the words of an early Christian profession of faith. The one God is the creator of all men. He cares for all his creatures as a father and wills that all men should be saved. There is only one mediator between God and men. It is he who makes known God's saving will to men and reconciles them with him, making peace between God and men; and this mediator is "the man Christ Jesus." He is capable of acting as our mediator because, as God's Son, he has the power to undertake this role, and as man he belongs to the human race and is therefore in a position to mediate.

What did this mediator do? He gave his life in our stead, to make atonement on behalf of the whole human race which had become subject to death. "The Son of man did not come to have service done him; he came to serve others and to give his life as a ransom for many" (Mk. 10:45). Jesus' death for all men on the cross is the "testimony" which God bore at the moment appointed for the fulfillment of his promises, "when the fullness of time had come" (Gal. 4:4). This is the message which he revealed to men. It is because they believe there is only one God and one mediator, Jesus Christ, that Christians are bound to pray for all mankind without exception. It is this, too, which forms the basis of their hope, their bold confidence, in including all men in their prayer, that they "may come to knowledge of the truth."

[7]I have been appointed a herald, an apostle, of this truth—I am not lying, I am telling the truth—as a teacher of the gentiles, in faith and truth.

Paul is the "herald" appointed to proclaim the gospel of God's universal salvific will to the whole world. He is the "apostle," God's authorized spokesman, appointed to make known the revelation of God's all-embracing salvific will and the saving activity of Jesus Christ the mediator to the gentiles and bring them to faith in God's revelation. With an assurance which is almost an oath—"I am not lying, I am telling the truth"—Paul insists that he has been commissioned by God and confirms what he has said, to ward off the attacks of the heretics who doubted his authority. The joyful pride in his words is clear, as he describes the glory of the office with which he was entrusted, and indeed of every office in the church which involves proclaiming the good news. This gives us some idea, too, of the obligations which a Christian has to welcome the message which is proclaimed with an open and willing spirit.

Rules of Behavior for Men and Women in the Liturgical Assembly (2:8–15)

[8]It is my wish that the men should offer prayer everywhere, raising up hands that are holy, free from anger and dispute.

Paul is particularly anxious that Christians should have the right attitude towards prayer. He tells us first of all how the men are to pray, "with hands that are holy." "Hands that are holy" symbolize a heart that is clean, sinless, and free from moral stain. It is from such a heart that their prayer must rise. In their prayer, they must be free from "anger and dispute"; they must live in peace with their brothers in Christ, without indulging in quarrels which are opposed to charity. Our Lord tells us in the Sermon on the Mount, "If you are bringing your gift to the altar and you remember there that your brother has something against you, leave your gift before the altar and go and be reconciled to your brother first. Then you can come and offer your gift" (Mt. 5:23f.). How can a man beg God for forgiveness, if he keeps hatred in his heart and refuses to forgive others? Jesus warns us, "When you stand praying, forgive anyone against whom you have some complaints, so that your Father in heaven will forgive you your sins too" (Mk. 11:25). Paul knows the heart of man; he knows that "anger and dispute" are the very sins which hinder prayer and the worship and praise of God in the case of men. That is why he warns them that they must pray with a pure and clean heart and one which is free from hatred or anger, when they say, "Forgive us our trespasses as we forgive those who trespass against us" (Mt. 6:12).

[9]Similarly, it is my wish that the women should adorn them-

selves with modesty and restraint in a becoming manner, not with braided hair, gold, precious stones, or costly clothing,
[10]*but with good works, as is expected of women who claim to worship God.*

The liturgical assembly also holds special dangers for women. Paul was probably moved to give these directions by abuses in the various local churches. A woman may easily be tempted to offend against the dignity of the liturgical celebration by exaggerated attention to her appearance. That is why Paul points out that the most suitable adornment for a religious woman consists, not in exaggerated attention to her physical appearance, but in a good Christian life and in activities which are in keeping with this. A woman's beauty should consist " not in her outward appearance, in braided hair, in golden bracelets, or extravagant clothes, but in the hidden features of her heart, in the beauty of a calm and peaceful spirit which is everlasting and beyond price in God's sight " (1 Pet. 3:3f.).

[11]*Women must learn in silence and submission.* [12]*I will not allow a woman to give instruction or lord it over her husband; they must remain silent.*

Continuing his admonitions, Paul forbids women to play a public part in the assembly; they must not give instruction or speak publicly. It had become customary in the Pauline churches such as Corinth for women who had the gift of prophecy to be allowed to speak in the liturgical assembly. However, this custom led to dangerous consequences. Such women easily neglected their housework and it seems there were efforts to throw off the yoke of submission to their husbands and give them orders. Paul wants women to be silent in the common assembly; they must not give instruction in public during the liturgical worship; instead they must be content " to learn in silence." It is for the men only to give instruction in the common assembly, while the women must be prepared to be taught. It is probable that there had been regrettable incidents in Christian communities which led Paul to insist on these regulations.

[13]*Adam was created first, and then Eve.* [14]*And Adam was not led astray; it was the woman who let herself be led away and fell into sin.*

In the efforts of some women to gain the upper hand over their husbands, Paul sees an offense against the order of creation. In his eyes, as he sees it expressed in the writings of the Old Testament, a woman is *subject to her husband*. He is led to this conclusion by two facts recounted in the Bible. According to the story of creation, Adam was created before his wife (Gen. 2:22). In the Jewish view, therefore, man is older than woman, and women are subject to men, because they are younger. Moreover, Eve was led astray personally by the serpent, while Adam merely followed his wife by giving his consent (Gen. 3:6, 17).

For Paul, these two facts prove that there is a certain hierarchy governing the relationship between a man and a woman in their common life. Of course, both men and women enjoy the same dignity in God's sight as human beings, and they both have the same share in the grace of Christ. In this there is no distinction. Moreover, this relationship between men and women must never be confused with a form of domination by a husband over his wife, which is an offense against God's will. On the contrary, husbands are bound to love their wives as their own flesh and blood (Eph. 5:28). God's sentence of condemnation after the fall makes it clear that husbands will often lord it over their wives in fact. However, it also implies that this must not be regarded as the order of things intended by God (Gen. 3:16).

[15]*Women will be saved by motherhood, if they persevere in faith and love and their own sanctification, together with self-discipline.*

The order of creation (Gen. 3:16) also shows us the task God has set for married women. This is the duty of *motherhood.* Paul refers explicitly to the fact that a woman must work out her salvation by fulfilling her duties as a mother. In this way, she enters into the scheme of things ordained by God himself. Of course, she must also practice the basic virtues of the Christian life, faith and love, as well as devoting herself to the work of her own sanctification and the exercise of Christian moderation. It seems likely that in this passage (2:11–15), Paul adopts a position in sharp contrast to that of the heretics in the community who rejected marriage (4:3) and gave a wrong explanation of the position of women in the Christian church. Paul is determined to maintain the dignity of Christian marriage and prove that the duties laid on Christian women by God lie in the home and within the family circle. It was not for them to play a public role in the celebration of the liturgy.

Office-Bearers (3:1–13)

The Qualifications of "Bishops" (3:1–7)

The first part of the section devoted to the organization of the church dealt with the celebration of the liturgy (2:1–15). The second part now deals with those who bear office in the community. Paul names for Timothy a whole series of qualifications which are necessary and must be demanded for the office of "bishops" (3:1–7) and deacons (3:8–13). These qualifications are concerned not so much with the particular duties of these officials as with the prerequisites necessary if a person is to be suitable for the office. The term "bishop" (= "overseer") in the pastoral epistles has not yet got the precise meaning it had in the church in the second century. Here, as in other passages of the New Testament, the term is used to describe the office of those who presided over a local church, the leaders of the local community, of whom there were more than one. Elsewhere in the New Testament they are described with the word "presbyter."

[1]*The saying that a man who aspires to the office of a bishop is hankering after a noble task is one which deserves our credence.*
[2]*A bishop must be free from fault, a man of one wife, sober, circumspect, virtuous, hospitable, and capable of teaching.* [3]*He must not be given to drunkenness or violence; instead, he should be unassuming, peaceful and free from avarice.*

With a formula which we have met before (see 1:15), Paul here introduces another quotation which exalts the *sublimity of the office* of leadership in the community. The verse lays special emphasis on the magnitude of the task involved. Leadership of a Christian community is a sacred and exalted ministry. That is why Paul is bound to demand certain qualifications; for office-bearers in the community he wants honorable men who are able to control themselves. In this respect, it is worth noting how he takes into account the state of the different communities from which the bearers of office are to be chosen, when prescribing the necessary qualifications. Paul is a prudent and experienced pastor of souls.

What are the qualities demanded in a leader of the community? First of all it is laid down in general that he should be "free from fault." If a man is to earn the trust of the community and be honored with it, his life must be free from stain. What this innocence of life implies in each different sphere is made clear by the enumeration of qualities which follows. He must be "a man of one wife." This must not be taken to mean only that his married life must be free from the slightest shadow of suspicion; it means that he must not have contracted a second marriage after the death of his wife. Paul expressly allows ordinary Christians to remarry, but he demands that those who are to lead the community should renounce this right. We could say that this is a first step towards the ideal of celibacy as the church imposed it at a later date on all those who bear office.

In addition, the leader of the community must be "sober." That is, he must be temperate in the use of wine and show himself circumspect in assessing circumstances and in all his decisions. His whole life must be honorable and above reproach. Hospitality towards strangers and one's brothers in Christ who are on their travels is a virtue which is demanded of Christians again and again in the New Testament. It goes without saying, therefore, that the head of the community must always keep open house for Christians who are on their travels or are in need of help. Teaching other Christians also forms part of the duties of the leader of the community. Therefore he must have a special talent for such work.

One who governs the community must not be given to drunkenness; he must not be a violent or quarrelsome man. Instead, he must be peace-loving and set an example of moderation and unselfishness.

[4]He must be a man who runs his own home well and keeps his children under control with all honor. [5]If a man is not able to run his own home, how can he be responsible for God's family? [6]He must not be a new convert, for fear he should become proud and fall prey to Satan's condemnation.

Paul is particularly emphatic about his demand that the family life of the leader of the community should be exemplary. In the early days, those who bore office in the church were married men; celibacy was introduced by the church only at a later date. If the head of the community is married, he must be able to prove in the narrow circle of his own family that he is a good head in his own household and that he is capable of training his own children in respect and obedience. If he is a failure at looking after his own family, he certainly cannot be trusted with a huge family like the Christian community, with all its spiritual and material needs.

The head of the community must not be a "new convert." Paul himself had already worked at Ephesus from A.D. 54–57 and established the church there. It is not surprising, therefore, that he should prescribe that those who are to lead the community should have had the faith and lived a Christian life for a longer period. The responsibilities of such an office are too great for a new convert; he is not yet firmly established in the faith and he aspires to an office of leadership without due consideration. Paul was an experienced pastor and a prudent judge of men; he knew that a new convert could easily be tempted to pride and vanity, if he was given charge of the community. If he succumbed to these passions, the devil would execute God's sentence of condemnation on him.

[7]He must also have a good name among those who are not of

our company, so that he will not be disgraced or fall prey to the wiles of Satan.

The last qualification that Paul demands is "a good name among those who are not of our company," among the Jews and pagans who were not members of the church. Paul often gives the same instructions to his churches and his disciples. A good name like this is even more important for the leaders of the church. If a man's early life was not free from blame, spiteful people could easily reveal it and use it to ruin the reputation of the head of the community. His position demands absolute innocence and purity; every stain on his life contains the danger of a relapse into the vices and passions which he has overcome. Such a stain may become a trap by which Satan and his accomplices will bring him to total destruction.

If we examine the qualifications that Paul demands of the leaders of the community, we see that he has in mind men of a very high degree of virtue and very firm faith in God. They must be prepared to obey God in all things and serve him in love. We should also note that Paul fails to mention any of the specifically human qualities which we so often look for, outstanding talent, eloquence, a sure touch, or organizing ability. For him the important qualification is the readiness, based on a true and firm faith, to obey God and serve him in love.

The Qualifications of Deacons (3:8–13)

Besides the office of a "bishop" as head of the community, the pastoral epistles also mention the diaconate. These "ministers" were responsible for the care of the poor, for preaching, and for the administration of baptism. Paul enumerates the qualities they must have.

[8]*Deacons must be honorable men in the same way; they must not be deceitful or given to immoderate indulgence in wine or sordid avarice.* [9]*They must be men who hold fast to the mystery of the faith with a pure conscience.* [10]*They, too, must first be put to the test and exercise their ministry only if they are without fault.*

It was the deacon's duty to distribute charity and alms and look after the poor. Consequently, they were entrusted with the community's money. That was why they had to be honorable in every way. People had to be able to rely on them to administer these sums honestly; the danger that they might make money for themselves dishonestly had to be excluded.

They must be men who "hold fast to *the mystery of the faith* with a pure conscience." By means of their preaching and the administration of baptism, together with their care for the poor, deacons shared in the pastoral ministry. Therefore, they had to know about "the mystery of the faith," so that they could proclaim it to others. This is the gospel of salvation through Jesus Christ which God the Father had kept hidden until it was revealed in Jesus Christ, so that it remained a "mystery." In addition, they must hold fast to this gospel with a "pure conscience," that is, one which is free from all stain. Nothing harms the faith so much as being championed by a man whose conscience is burdened with sin.

The early life and the moral conduct of the men to whom the office of diaconate is to be entrusted, with its absolute need of reliability, must be *put to the test* during a period of probation. It is only when the blameless character of their previous lives has been proved that they should exercise their ministry.

[11]*The women, too, must be honorable, not given to slander; they must be sober and reliable in every way.*

Women are mentioned in the middle of the list of qualities demanded of deacons. Is the reference to the deacons' wives (in which case we should expect the words " Their women folk "), or to women who held office in the church as the deacons did? Such were the " deaconesses " whom Paul mentions later (5:9–16), one of whom, " our sister Phoebe," is named in Romans 16:1 as " the deaconess of the church at Cenchrae." The deaconesses assisted in the charitable activities of the community, so that their duties were important. That was why they had to be perfectly " honorable." They must not be prone to slander and the sins of the tongue, into which some women easily fall. In addition, they must be completely trustworthy in every other way.

[12]*The deacons must be men of one wife and good heads to their own households and their children.* [13]*Those who have performed this office well attain an exalted rank and great confidence in their faith in Jesus Christ.*

Like a " bishop," the head of the community, a deacon too must have been married only once. He must prove his suitability for the office of a deacon by his exemplary family life, by bringing up his children carefully, and running his own home well. In this way he will give the community good example.

If a deacon is faithful to his duty and " performs his office well," he will attain an " exalted rank." Does this refer to some rank of honor within the community to which the deacon may rise despite his position as the servant of others? Or does it refer to the possibility of ascending to the office of " bishop " and leader of the community? In 3:1 this is described as an " exalted office." Such fidelity to duty gives a deacon great confidence on the day of judgment, when he must give an account of his stewardship. As he looks forward to God's sentence, he must be full of confidence, not on the ground of what he has accomplished personally or his own merits, but on the ground of his faith in Jesus Christ.

The qualifications that Paul demands of a deacon are similar to those demanded of a " bishop." However, there are two qualities necessary for a " bishop " which are characteristic of his office and which are omitted in the case of deacons. A bishop must be " capable of teaching," and he must not be " a new convert." For the subordinate role of the diaconate, therefore, Paul demands candidates who are mature in virtue. They must be outstanding in the community for their good Christian lives and they must be prepared to submit to God in service and love.

The Reason for These Regulations; the Sublimity of the Divine Mystery Which Is Entrusted to the Church (3:14-16)

[14]*I write this to you in the hope of being able to come to you very soon.*

In keeping with the plans he had in mind even when sending this letter, Paul wanted to return to Timothy at Ephesus *as soon as possible.* He realized, however, that his journey might be postponed for one reason or another. That was why he gave his representative instructions concerning the organization of the community, the liturgical assembly (2:1–15), and the choice of office-bearers (3:1–13). The charge of his churches occupied Paul constantly. It never left him, even when he was far from them in person. His intimate relationship with Timothy, "my own son in the faith" (1:2), moved him to send him detailed instructions, so that he would know how "he should behave in God's house."

[15]*Should I delay, however, you must realize how a person is expected to behave in God's house which is the church of the living God, the pillar and foundation of the truth.*

There is another reason too. Paul's vision widens. The organization of the community which he has just prescribed (2:1—3:13) is not intended only for Timothy in Ephesus. The whole church in Asia Minor now stands before his eyes, with all its different local communities. The regulations he has made concerning the community and the church in Ephesus are valid for them too. In an image which occurs in other passages of the New Testament also, the Christian community, the church of the living God, is called "God's house." Therefore, God who possesses the fullness of life and is the source of all life lives in the community. He is never far from Christians; "where two or three are gathered together in my name I am there in their midst" (Mt. 18:20). What a consolation and a joy this should be for Christians! And what a heavy responsibility! The God who lives in the community as in a temple is an all-holy God. He will not allow his house to be desecrated or destroyed. "God will destroy anyone who destroys his temple; God's temple is holy and you are this temple" (1 Cor. 3:17).

Paul now uses a different metaphor and mentions two essential characteristics of the church which come to the same thing in reality. The church is the " pillar and foundation of the truth." The church has been established in the world by God like a pillar or a foundation on which his revelation rests; there it can be seen by all men. The church is the infallible and indestructible repository and protectress of the truth revealed by God. The truth is in good and safe keeping in the church and from the church it shines forth to enlighten the darkness of error.

16*And without doubt, the mystery of piety is something sublime. He was revealed in human flesh, justified in spirit, revealed to the angels and proclaimed to the nations; he was believed in the world and taken up into glory.*

The centerpiece of the truth revealed by God is the " mystery of piety," Jesus Christ himself. These six brief phrases refer to him, although he is not mentioned by name. They are an attempt to sum up the mystery of Jesus Christ in a concise formula. It is probable that they are taken from an early Christian hymn, such as may have been sung in the churches of the time. The mystery of Christ is presented in three pairs of contrasting phrases, flesh-spirit, the world of the angels-the world of the nations, the world of earth-the glory of heaven.

The contrast " flesh-spirit " is intended to bring out the human and divine nature of Christ. Christ's " revelation " in the " flesh " is contrasted with his " justification in the spirit." The " revelation in the flesh " is the incarnation. Christ, who had existed before the world with God, entered into this world and became man by taking human nature. He was justified by the " spirit " and his divine nature was proved beyond doubt. This was accomplished by the miracles he worked during his life, by his resurrection, and by his exaltation at the Father's right hand. Through the "spirit," God showed the whole world that Jesus who had been put to death on the cross as a criminal was really "the holy and the just one" (Acts 3:14). As a result of his resurrection, which was accomplished in the spirit (see Rom. 8:11), Jesus Christ shares God's divine being even as man.

The second contrast, "revealed to the angels and proclaimed to the nations," refers to the victory won by Christ who has ascended into heaven, a victory which concerns the world of angels as well as his dominion over the whole world of men. Christ was "revealed" to the angels and presented to them in visible human form as he ascended into heaven. Now they adore him and are completely subject to him as their lord. This glorification in the sight of the angels is matched by the proclamation of Christ among the "nations" in his kingdom on earth. Wherever the good news of the salvation Jesus Christ brings is proclaimed among the nations, his right to kingship over the whole of creation is also affirmed.

The third pair of opposites, "believed in the world and taken up into glory," describes the victory which Christ who has been exalted in glory has won in this world as a result of the world's acceptance of him by faith, and in the world to come as a result of his sharing in God's glory. There he is eternally surrounded by this glory, as he sits on his Father's right hand. The victory won by the glorified Christ is constantly proclaimed in the world, wherever men open their hearts to the preaching of the gospel as a message of salvation, and arrive at real faith in Jesus. It is similarly proclaimed in heaven by the fact that he is seated at God's right hand and has been admitted into the abyss of divine light.

In the hymn which Paul here makes his own, the early Christian church expresses its belief in the eternal Son of God who entered into this world and became man. After his earthly life and his crucifixion, he was exalted at God's right hand as the Lord of the universe, of the angels, and of all mankind. " Without doubt, the mystery of piety is something sublime," so sublime, so incomprehensible that mere men cannot grasp it. Together with the angels they can only cast themselves down in humble adoration before the eternal Son of God, who became man and now sits at God's right hand.

THE HERETICS AND THEIR INNOVATIONS (4:1–11)

Paul has come to the end of his instructions on how the church should be run and he closes this section with a joyful hymn of praise to Christ. He now returns once more to the struggle that Timothy will have to carry on against the heretics, which he has already spoken about (1:3–20). The proper regulation of the life of the community, the expansion of its organization by the institution of "bishops" and deacons, and the preservation of the church from false doctrines are the principal tasks which Paul recommends to his disciple in this letter. He has already spoken of the heretics' doctrinal views (1:3–20); here he deals especially with the innovations which they tried to introduce into the Christian way of life. He mentions the prohibition of marriage and their demand for abstinence from certain kinds of food (4:1–5). Finally, he warns Timothy that he must give an example of genuinely Christian living to the whole community (4:6–11).

The Prohibition of Marriage and Certain Foods (4:1–5)

[1]*The Spirit says explicitly that in later days many will abandon the faith and fall prey to false spirits and the teachings of devils . . .*

Paul now gives us a fresh description of the heretics who had made their appearance in Ephesus, based on various traits which were characteristic of them. The appearance of such persons should not come as a surprise to Timothy and the other

Christians. God's *Spirit* himself had foretold by means of people endowed with the gift of prophecy that the Christian church would suffer many apostasies from the faith, in the last period of time, that is, the period before the second coming of Christ. Paul does not tell us the names of these prophets and we have no further information concerning the circumstances in which they made their predictions. From the very first, the early church held fast to the belief that the period preceding the second coming of Christ would be marked by bitter *struggles* concerning the teaching of the gospel, and the *apostasy* of many Christians. Our Lord himself warned his disciples, " Let no one lead you astray. Many will come in my name and say, Here I am, and many people will be deceived " (Mk. 13:5f.). " False messiahs and false prophets will appear. They will perform signs and miracles, to deceive even the elect, if it were possible " (Mk. 13:22).

Paul also speaks of this apostasy. When he was saying good-bye to the presbyters from Ephesus at Miletus, he foretold it just as definitely: " I know that when I am gone, fierce wolves will force their way among you and will not spare the flock. Men will arise from your own ranks bearing a false message, in search of disciples who will follow them " (Acts 20:29f.). The seeds of the heresy which will lead to such apostasy " in later days " are already *present*. The heretics who have already made their appearance in Ephesus are the forerunners of a world of spirits who are God's enemies and are intent on destroying Christ's church and undermining the work accomplished by the apostles. They have abandoned the truths of the Christian faith for " false spirits and the teachings of devils." There is something sinister about these efforts of the demons to combat Christ and his truth. Like Paul, we must have no illusions; we must take a realistic view of the powers of evil. Consequently, we must be extremely vigilant; " the devil goes about like a roaring lion, looking for someone to devour " (1 Pet. 5:8). God's Spirit, however, has warned the church, so that it will not be taken by surprise or led astray.

2. . . *led astray by people who are hypocrites and liars, whose consciences carry the mark of a branding-iron.*

There are two signs which show that these heretics are the instruments of diabolical powers; they are hypocrites and liars. Their preaching and the sanctity of which they make such a display are not genuine. Their sanctity is false; it is only apparent. Their manner of speaking and living gives no indication of what they are really like. " They come in sheep's clothing, but they are ravenous wolves within " (Mt. 7:15).

Their " consciences carry the mark of a branding-iron." In those days, slaves were marked on their bodies with a searing-iron, to indicate whom they belonged to. Heretics are branded in their consciences in the same way. This mark consists in the fact that they are enslaved to sin; they are in bondage to secret sins, especially avarice and selfishness (6:3). Of course, they try to conceal this by the severe religious and moral demands they make. Paul now pronounces his severest condemnation on them; they are the instruments of the devils, of Satan.

However, Timothy and the rest of the church must not be disturbed by their appearance. The advent of heretics and the apostasy of many Christians are not an example of blind fate imposing itself upon the community; such happenings, too, have a place in God's plan of salvation. The life of the church runs its course securely in the protective and loving hands of God the

Father. Nothing can happen to it, nothing can destroy its peace, without God being aware of it, even if Satan sends his instruments and leads some people astray. Nothing can happen without God's permission or contrary to his plan of salvation. It is this consciousness which encourages, comforts, and strengthens the church, even in its greatest needs.

3a*They forbid marriage and impose abstinence from certain foods . . .*

The heretics pretended to stand for a very severe and mortified conception of the Christian life. They demanded the renunciation of marriage and abstinence from (certain) foods.

These demands give us some idea what kind of heresy was involved. The prohibition of certain types of food must be regarded as having some connection with Jewish laws concerning ritual purity which forbade eating certain types of food. The prohibition of marriage, on the other hand, is quite foreign to the Jewish mentality. It must come from gnostic influences. Gnosticism distinguished so sharply between body and soul, the material world and the world of the spirit, and separated them so much that the earthly world of matter was regarded as being something opposed to God. Consequently, the gnostics maintained that the way to union with God lay in liberating the soul from all contact with matter. They preached renunciation of marriage as a matter of obligation; it was the only way to achieve freedom from the material world. Similar heresies were widespread in other early Christian churches.

We see, therefore, that even rigorous asceticism can be heretical, if it deviates from Christ's teaching. It is heretical to maintain, for example, that we can gain access to God or earn the right to eternal salvation by our own unaided efforts in observing various severe precepts. What we are bound to do in reality is to accept with all humility the forgiveness of sins and the grace which Christ has merited and offers to us.

[3b] *. . . which God has made to be enjoyed with gratitude by those who have faith and have recognized the truth.* [4]*Everything that God has made is good and nothing is to be rejected, if it is enjoyed with gratitude;* [5]*for then it is sanctified by God's word and by prayer.*

This heresy offends against the order of creation established by God. Paul emphatically lays down the vitally important principle, " Everything that God has made is good." Every created thing comes from the hand of God the creator. That is why we are told, at the end of the description of creation, " And God looked at everything he had made, and it was very good " (Gen. 1:31). God's creation, which has been redeemed by Jesus Christ, is free from all taint, as God himself revealed clearly to Peter in a vision. Christ redeemed the world from Satan's power and the power of sin; he has already established his kingdom in it and at the end of time he will bring this to its perfect achievement. In this redeemed world there is no longer anything which is unclean. Christians who have learned to recognize this truth can enjoy all the gifts of creation to the full.

The use of God's gifts is subject to only one condition; they must be accepted and enjoyed " with gratitude." On three different occasions, Paul expressly mentions grace before meals as a condition for the proper enjoyment of all the gifts God has given us to preserve our life. Grace before meals was a valuable custom inherited from the Jews which the early Christians adopted from the chosen people of the Old Testament and observed faithfully. As had been the case with the chosen people of Israel, it was taken for granted in the first Christian communities that no one would ever eat a piece of bread or drink a glass of wine without giving thanks to the Giver of all good gifts. Jesus had been scrupulous in observing the custom of offering praise to God before meals and thanking him afterwards, and the early church was equally scrupulous in saying grace. When something which is a gift from God is hallowed by saying grace over it, which consists in " God's word " (an inspired text from the Old Testament) and a " prayer " (an expression of praise), it is no longer unclean. In such a case, the prohibition of certain foods imposed by the heretics is completely meaningless. This shows us how seriously Paul and the early Christians took the custom of saying grace, as Jesus had taught them. We ourselves are often far from imitating their behavior.

Correct Christian Practice (4:6–11)

6*If you make this known to the brethren, you will be an outstanding servant of Jesus Christ, nourished by the words of the faith and the excellent doctrine which you have taken as your guide.*

Paul once more addresses Timothy personally. In contrast to the heretics, he must keep the Christian community on the right path and call upon them to make proper use of God's gifts, including marriage and food. By so doing, he will show that his teaching is based on Christian revelation, and that the " words of the faith and the excellent doctrine " of Jesus Christ are his spiritual nourishment. After the example of Jesus Christ, he will show that God's will and God's revelation in the gospel is his food. This is the only teaching which can serve as his guide in his life as a Christian; for him, there is no other source of truth.

If anyone wishes to be " Christ's servant," he can have only one form of spiritual nourishment, the " word of the faith "; no merely human concept or precepts imposed by men can be of service, no matter how austere the ideal they represent. He can have only one rule of life, the " excellent doctrine " of Jesus Christ, as it is made known to us by the mouth of the church.

7a*Reject unholy old wives' tales!*

Paul contemptuously refers to the heretics' teaching as " unholy old wives' tales." They substitute their " legends and interminable genealogies " (1 : 4) for God's revelation. What a contrast these are to the " excellent doctrine " of Jesus Christ which alone can govern Timothy's life and behavior. This is the idle chatter of " old wives' tales." There is no room for discussion in this matter. Timothy must take a firm stand—clear and uncompromising rejection.

7b*Exercise yourself rather in holiness.* 8*Bodily exercise is not much use; holiness, on the other hand, is useful in all circumstances because it carries with it a promise for this life and for the next.* 9*This saying deserves our credence and a warm welcome.*

Paul has refuted the severe ascetical practices of the heretics, including the prohibition of marriage and abstinence from certain foods (4:3). Timothy's ascetical practices must be of a completely different kind. He must devote himself to growing in holiness. His whole life must become an ever clearer example of Christian teaching. In all the concrete circumstances of his life, he must try to give better expression to the new being, the new life he enjoys as a Christian, and to live up to it. In his behavior and in all his actions, he must proclaim ever more clearly Christ's essential message, love of God and one's neighbor. Paul loves to use images drawn from sport to illustrate the Christian life. In this passage, he uses an expression drawn from the Greek "gymnasium," a place set aside for contests and physical training. "Exercise" such as this, which is aimed at increasing intimacy with God and greater holiness, is better and worth far more than any physical "gymnastics." Holiness carries with it a promise of "life" even for this earth, but especially for the world to come. Paul was familiar with the "physical exercises" which took place in the arenas of old. He gives them some recognition, but he also realizes that they are "not worth much." The most they can produce is fitness and health in this earthly life. Exercising oneself in holiness is far more important by comparison. This carries with it the promise of the greatest and most beautiful gift of salvation a man can receive, the "eternal life" which is to come.

10*It is for this that we labor and struggle, because we have put our hope in the living God who is the saviour of all men, but especially of those who have faith.* 11*Teach this and bring it home to people.*

It is the thought of the great gift of salvation, eternal life, which enables Paul and his fellow workers to bear all the hardships and toils of life. In the same way, an athlete in a race or a boxer in the ring does his utmost to win the prize of victory and renounces everything which could hinder him. Of course, a Christian's hope of attaining the prize of victory is not based on his own achievements or his own training, on his own efforts or his own struggles. The living God alone can and will fulfill his promises; it is his wish that all men should be saved (2:3f.), and he gives special proof of his universal salvific will to Christians. Paul calls upon his disciple to do his share in this struggle for the gift of eternal life. These are the instructions he must give to his church.

INSTRUCTIONS TO TIMOTHY CONCERNING HIS OFFICE (4:12—6:2)

In the second part of his letter (2:1—3:16), Paul gave Timothy general directions concerning the proper organization of liturgical worship, and he also enumerated the qualifications which must be demanded of those who are to bear office in the community. In the fourth part, he now gives him personal instructions dealing with the exercise of his own office in the church at Ephesus. The norms that Paul lays down here are intended to provide for the proper government of the church. First of all, he exhorts Timothy in a general way to lead an exemplary life and be enthusiastic about his work (4:12–16). This is followed by directions for dealing correctly with the various age-groups within the community (5:1f.) and instructions concerning widows and the rules governing their position (5:3–16). Finally, Paul speaks of presbyters (5:17–25) and the treatment of slaves (6:1f.).

An Exhortation to Lead an Exemplary Life and Be Zealous (4:12–16)

Verses 12–16 are once more addressed to Timothy personally. The number and variety of these brief exhortations, together with the repetition of the imperative form of the verb, show the great love and anxiety that his spiritual father (1:2) felt for him.

12*You must allow no one to think little of you because of your* *youth; on the contrary, you must be an example to the faithful in word and deed, in love, in faith, and in purity.*

This passage makes it clear that Timothy was a young man. About thirteen years previously he had been admitted among Paul's closest collaborators. At the time this letter was sent, we can be sure he was in his thirties. Had his lack of years given rise to certain difficulties in the exercise of his office as head of the community? It seems that this is what we must conclude from Paul's warning, when he tells him, "You must allow no one to think little of you because of your youth." No one likes to take orders, instructions, or discipline from a young man. Moreover, it was customary for older men to be put in charge of Christian communities. Paul, however, was quite conscious of the reasons he had for putting Timothy in charge, despite his youth. Therefore he stands protectingly over his representative and encourages him in the exercise of his office. What he lacks in years, he must make up for by his exemplary life, in his enthusiastic preaching of God's word, in his dealings with all the members of the community, in the uprightness of his self-sacrificing life, in the firmness of his deep faith, and the purity of his whole heart. Paul feels genuine concern for his youthful representative and he is anxious to bolster his authority and confirm his position in a sensible way. Both men were united by their deep love for the community.

13 *Until I come, devote yourself to public reading, to exhorting, and to instructing.*

Paul has already told Timothy that he will come as soon as possible (3:14). Until he comes, Timothy must exercise his office faithfully and without wavering, despite his youth. He must be of service to the community by " publicly reading " from the Old Testament in the liturgical assembly. The early church adopted the custom of reading from the books of the Old Testament from the liturgy of the Jewish synagogue. This was soon followed by readings from the writings of the apostles and the gospels. This reading from the scripture was accompanied by an *exhortation* and an *instruction* delivered by the head of the community or some preacher who enjoyed the gifts of the Spirit. It was this ministry of reading, instructing, and exhorting that Timothy was bound to perform faithfully until Paul came. From the very beginning, Christians have heard God's word read aloud from the writings of the Old and New Testaments. God's call goes out to them continually, just as God speaks to us today through this epistle.

14*Do not neglect the gift of grace which is in you, which was conferred on you as the result of prophecy and the laying on of the presbyters' hands.*

In addition, Paul reminds his disciple and fellow worker of the " gift of grace " which he received when his office was conferred upon him by the imposition of the Apostle's hands and those of the whole college of presbyters. As in 1:18, Paul refers to the prophecy concerning Timothy which was made as he was looking for a representative on his departure from Ephesus. Timothy was pointed out by the revelations of people who were endowed with the Spirit, as the man chosen by God for the position. Together with the presbyterium, the college of elders, Paul then laid hands on him and conferred on him the grace of office. This was, of course, a permanent gift which was given him to enable him to fulfill his task as head of the church. It qualified him to exercise the many different forms of service associated with his office, among which were " reading publicly, exhorting, and teaching." Timothy, therefore, was bound to take constant care that the grace of office he had received did not remain sterile or ineffective. It came to him as a gift from God and was intended to be used. Despite his youthfulness, therefore, he must administer the office entrusted to him confidently. His only anxiety must be to ensure that God's gift to him is not neglected. God's gifts always imply a commission, an obligation to exercise them.

15*Be careful of this and devote yourself to it completely, so that*
the progress you make may be clear to everybody. 16*Attend to*
yourself and to the teaching of the faith and persevere in it. If
you do that, you will save yourself and those who hear you.

Paul's advice becomes shorter and more insistent. Timothy must take special care to lead an exemplary life, based on trust in the grace of office he has received. He must immerse himself more and more in the teaching of Christianity and put it into practice ever more perfectly in his own life. Then his " progress " will be clear to everyone in the community and they will obey him readily. He must devote himself entirely to fulfilling the duties of his office and pay great attention to the conduct of his own life, while preserving the doctrine which has been entrusted to him pure and unadulterated. His " salvation," his eternal destiny and that of the community he is responsible for, depend on the way he watches over himself, on the example he sets in his life, and on how he preaches the good news to others.

Correct Treatment of the Various Age-Groups (5:1–2)

[1]*Do not speak roughly to an elderly man. Instead, exhort him like a father; speak to younger men as your brothers,* [2]*to elderly women as mothers, and to younger women, in all modesty, as your sisters.*

In a few words Paul describes for his representative the basic attitude which should determine his behavior and his conduct with the various age-groups in the community. There is no doubt that Timothy is the head of the church and possesses the authority which goes with this office. Indeed, Paul in this letter is completely behind him and clearly intends to confirm his position. However, the Christian community is not and must not be regarded merely as an organization within which Timothy wields his authority. Above everything else, it is a great *family* which must be filled with the spirit of genuine love. Jesus himself called his disciples his brothers, sisters, and mothers, and he taught them to regard themselves as a great family. The family spirit of the primitive church at Jerusalem is quite clear from the account we have in the Acts of the Apostles. The faithful had " one heart and soul."

Timothy, too, must regard the community entrusted to him as his family. He must treat them as people with whom he is united by the same love and reverence as he has for his own parents and sisters. Despite his lack of years, therefore, he will not address an older man harshly, even if he must reproach and correct him. He will treat him with all respect, like a father, and he will treat an older woman as his mother. He will approach younger men and women as his brothers and sisters.

In his dealings with younger women especially he will be tactful and reserved, and show due respect and modesty.

Widows (5:3–16)

Because of their desperate plight, widows were specially recommended to the protection of the chosen people even by the law of the Old Testament. The early Christian church, too, showed loving care for them from the very beginning. There was no such thing as public social assistance or public provision for women who had lost their husbands. They were without relatives, and those who declined to remarry usually found themselves in difficult circumstances and suffered great want. In his instructions to Timothy concerning the proper exercise of office, Paul now deals with these Christians. It is important and very significant that Timothy should be specially recommended to care for the poorest of the poor, widows and slaves (6:1f.).

From the explanations that Paul gives we see that he uses the term "widow" in different senses. "Widows" in one passage are women who have lost their husbands and have not remarried, but still have children and grandchildren. They have some relatives, therefore, who are bound to care for them (5:4, 8). From these must be distinguished the "widows" in the community who have no relatives whatever and are completely alone and bereft of all means (5:3, 5). A third group of "widows" is made up of those women in the community who were engaged in works of charity. For these, Paul prescribes special qualifications (5:9–16), just as he had done for "bishops" and deacons (3:1–13).

The Care of Widows (5:3–8)

3Honor widows, if they are really widows.

In conscious imitation of the terminology of the fourth commandment, Paul prescribes that widows should be honored. This does not mean only that Timothy should welcome such widows with respect and show them external marks of honor as a mother (5:2); it means that he must give these poor women material support. Of course, this presupposes that they are really widows, women who have refused to remarry and have no one who is bound to care for them, so that they are alone and destitute in the community. Genuinely Christian love of one's neighbor must show itself by deeds in the case of these women and make their lot easier. Where real love exists in a community, it must show itself above all in the treatment of widows, these poor helpless women who have no means of support.

4*If a widow has children or grandchildren, they must be taught to fulfill their duty as children towards the members of their own household first, and recompense their own parents; this is pleasing in God's sight.*

Paul now defines the term " widow " more clearly. He says that *widows who have a family,* that is, children and grandchildren, must not be supported by the community. In this case, the obligation to support them rests on their children and grandchildren. They are bound to them by ties of blood, family relationship, and filial piety. By supporting them, they can show their gratitude to their parents and grandparents. Moreover, God has expressly imposed this obligation in the fourth commandment. If children and grandchildren have an obligation imposed by God towards their parents who are widowed, there is no need for the charitable intervention of the community on their behalf.

5*A woman who is really a widow and alone has set her hope in God and she perseveres day and night in prayer and tears.*

With widows who have relatives who are bound to support them, Paul contrasts those who are " really widows." Their state is characterized by the fact that they are alone and abandoned and live a life completely dependent on God. Such women have been proved by suffering and in their loneliness they consecrate their lives to God. Like the holy widow Anna (Lk. 2:36f), they are intimately united with him in constant prayer. It is for such widows that the community must make provision.

[6]*If she lives a dissolute life, she is dead, although she is still alive.*

If a widow tries to drown her sorrow by living a wanton and sinful life, indulging in the world's pleasures to the full, she is dead, as far as the Christian community is concerned. She no longer lives in union with Christ and she has lost the true life. She has the name of being alive, but she is dead (Rev. 3:1). Consequently, she has also spurned the right to the loving care of the community. Paul was an experienced pastor and he knew that even in Christian communities there were people who only had the name of being alive. In reality they were dead because they had dissolved their union with Jesus Christ who is life (Jn. 11:25).

[7]*Bring this home to them, that they may be without fault.* [8]*Anyone who does not care for his own relatives, and especially those who are members of the same household, has denied the faith and is worse than a pagan.*

Paul calls on Timothy to make these principles known to the community. They must allow their behavior and their treatment of widows to be guided by them. In this connection, Paul returns once more to something he had mentioned previously (5:4), moved perhaps by bitter experience. With sharp words he insists that the obligation of supporting widows rests primarily on their relatives. This obligation precedes any obligation the community has in their regard. If their relatives neglect this obligation, *they deny the faith* by their action. They still have the name of being Christians, but in practice they have abandoned the faith. They have fallen lower even than the pagans who have no knowledge of Christ or of the obligation of charity. They at least allowed themselves to be guided by reverence and filial love towards their parents, as we see so often in antiquity. Loveless treatment of those who are "members of the same household," refusal to support or help one's relatives in need imply apostasy from the faith in practice. Paul's teaching is perfectly clear. It recalls to our minds an obligation which even many Christians no longer wish to acknowledge.

The Office of Widows (5:9–16)

Paul now turns immediately to a third class of widows, without making any effort to underline the transition of thought. The context makes it clear that these widows were engaged in charitable activities among the community. Consequently, their names were entered on a special list. Like the "bishops" (3:2–7) and deacons (3:8–13), these widows held a particular office in the community. Therefore, certain qualifications were necessary before they could be appointed and have their names put on the list.

9 *Only a woman who is at least sixty years old and has been faithful to one husband can be entered on the list of widows.*

10 *She must have a reputation for good deeds, bringing up children, showing hospitality, washing the feet of the saints, caring for the afflicted, and dedicating herself to all kinds of good works.*

Paul expressly mentions three qualifications for widows who were active in the *service of the community*. The first is the age required. The reasons for this are given at length in the verses which follow. A widow must be over sixty years of age. This ensures that widows will be experienced and reliable persons. Younger widows had been a source of bitter experience in the past (5:11–15). An additional requirement is that they should have been married only once. By renouncing a second marriage, they kept faith with their dead husbands even beyond the grave. The third qualification that Paul mentions is the proof of a genuinely Christian life which consists in the practice of various works of charity. Their office in the community was concerned especially with works of charity. Such a duty could only be entrusted to women who had already proved themselves in their former lives by their good deeds and had earned a good name in the community.

As an example of such *charitable* deeds, Paul mentions bringing up children. He does not say whether this refers to their own children or the children of others, that is, orphans. Hospitality is also mentioned. This was very important in the early days of the church, because of the big number of wandering preachers and Christians who had been driven from their homes by persecution. "Washing the feet of the saints" is cited as a further example. This does not mean only that they must have a name for giving strangers a warm welcome; it also implies readiness to show unselfish and humble service towards all the

" saints," that is, all Christians. It includes, moreover, willingness to come to the aid of others in difficult circumstances and undertake any good work.

There is a fourth requirement which is not mentioned expressly; it can be clearly inferred from the description contained in the verses which follow. Such widows must renounce any further marriage. The inclusion of a woman's name in the list of widows was regarded as a form of betrothal to Christ (5 : 11f.). Even in the earliest days of the church, women played an important role in the service of the community. What Paul really requires of the widows who share in the charitable activities of the community is a mature personality which has been proved by a genuinely Christian life. They must be capable of practicing a charity inspired by their Christian faith and of consecrating their whole lives to this ministry.

[11]*On the other hand, you must turn younger widows away; if they feel the impulses of their passions, in opposition to Christ, they will want to marry again.* [12]*They then bear a sentence of condemnation, because they have violated their first loyalty.* [13]*At the same time, they learn idleness, as they run about from house to house, and not only are they idle, they are also gossipers and inquisitive and say things they should not say.*

Paul now gives the reasons why Timothy must exclude *young widows* from this ministry. In their case, earthly love may easily be stirred once more. This estranges them from Christ, so that they try to marry again. In this way, they break their pledge to Christ, although they have consecrated themselves to him, probably by a promise or even an oath taken on their admission to this office. They violate their " first loyalty " and incur God's condemnation. The duties of the widows' ministry could, moreover, be a great source of danger for young widows. The house visiting which was necessary could lead to idleness cloaked under an appearance of activity. It could also be an occasion for inordinate gossiping, interfering, and all kinds of sins of the tongue. To counteract these dangers, Paul as an experienced pastor and a shrewd judge of human nature instructs his disciple to exclude young widows from this ministry. Paul's feet are firmly planted on solid ground. He knows the dangers which threaten Christians in this world. That is why he is so careful even in choosing the widows who are to engage in ministering to the community.

14*It is my wish that the younger widows should marry and have children. They should look after their own households and so give our opponent no opportunity for speaking badly about us.*
15*Some have already turned aside to follow Satan.*

Young widows should *remarry,* do their duty as mothers, and look after their own homes. If these instructions of Paul are followed, there will be no danger of the church being slandered by its "opponent," the Jews or gentiles who were hostile to Christianity. They will have no opportunity for speaking badly about it. It is possible that Paul was prompted to give these instructions by various events in different local churches. He was speaking from a completely different viewpoint when he advised widows in another letter, "They will do well if they remain as I am" (1 Cor. 7:8); in other words, if they do not enter on another marriage. Paul placed a life of celibacy and virginity above married life, but he realized that his advice was not valid for everybody or in all circumstances.

Bitter experiences in the case of young widows who had abandoned the right road and followed Satan moved Paul to insist on these norms. Young widows had been led astray by heretics and abandoned the rule of faith and morals, so that they fell away to Satan.

[16]*If a woman who is a Christian has widows depending on her, she should care for them and not burden the community, so that it can care for those who are really widows.*

At the end of his discussion of the ministry of widows, Paul adds a remark on their *upkeep*. The reference is no longer clear to us. In an earlier passage (5:4), he had spoken of the obligation of a woman to support her widowed relatives. It seems, however, that the situation he has in mind here is different. He is probably thinking of a particular case in which a number of the widows engaged in ministering to the community lived together in the house of a wealthy Christian. If this woman has the means, she should provide for the widows who live with her. Then they will not be a burden to the community which is bound to care for those who are really friendless and destitute (5:3, 5).

We should note how anxious Paul is about the widows in the community who are impoverished and alone. We are told of the early church in Jerusalem (Acts 4:32f.) that "the multitude of the faithful had one heart and one soul and no one claimed that his possessions were his own; on the contrary, they held everything in common." Paul was anxious that this should be true of Ephesus, too, and should be demonstrated in the care taken of widows. The whole church must form a community of genuine brotherly love.

Presbyters (5:17–25)

Paul now gives instructions for another group of persons in the church at Ephesus. These were the presbyters or "elders." They were office-bearers who presided over the community at Ephesus and in other churches of Asia Minor as a college. As Paul's representative, Timothy was entrusted with the supreme control of all these local churches. In this passage, he is given instructions on how the presbyters are to be paid and the maintenance of ecclesiastical discipline among them. Paul had already mentioned them (4:14), when he reminded Timothy of the day when he laid hands on him, together with the college of presbyters. It is clear that their office is identical with that of the "bishops" (3:1–7). Paul makes it clear in the directions he gives that he personally had the highest regard for the presbyters. He was anxious to protect their honor and to ensure that their offenses would be judged impartially. He also made the appointment of a presbyter dependent upon serious and mature consideration.

17*The presbyters who are good superiors must be regarded as having earned double recognition, especially if they have spent themselves in preaching and teaching.* 18*Scripture says: "You shall not muzzle the ox which is threshing," and "The laborer is worthy of his hire."*

Paul is anxious that presbyters who have been faithful in performing their duty as heads of the community should be regarded as *having earned double recognition.* This should be so, particularly if they have dedicated themselves to proclaiming the word in preaching and instruction. "Double recognition" means a higher degree of esteem and respect, but also a correspondingly more generous provision for their upkeep. They should be paid a bigger income, according to the amount of work they have to do and the responsibility they bear. Paul gives two different reasons for the community's obligation to provide for the upkeep of their superiors, preachers, and instructors. He interprets a saying of scripture (Deut. 25:4) in a metaphorical sense, to explain their obligations to the community. The ox which pulls the threshing sledge and picks up ears of corn with its mouth must not be muzzled to stop it doing this; the work it is doing is hard. In the same way, those who preside over the community and spend themselves in its service have a claim to receive their upkeep from the community. Paul also quotes an expression used by Jesus himself which was familiar to the early Christians from the preaching of the gospel. Both Luke and Matthew included it in their gospels (Lk. 10:7; Mt. 10:10).

The right which those who bear office in the church have to their upkeep is based on the authority of the sacred writings of both the Old and the New Testament and on the words of Jesus himself. Paul is interested even in their material well-being in the community. In another passage he tells us, "The Lord, too, instructed those who preach the gospel to live by the gospel" (1 Cor. 9:14).

[19]*Admit no charge against a presbyter unless it is supported by two or three witnesses.* [20]*Correct those who are at fault in the presence of all, so as to inspire fear in the others.* [21]*I adjure you before God and Christ Jesus and the angels who are chosen: Follow these rules and avoid being partial.*

In this passage Paul gives important instructions for the maintenance of church discipline as far as the presbyters are concerned. The rule that no charge could be brought against a presbyter unless it was supported by two or three witnesses is in keeping with the provisions of the Old Testament law and the earliest Christian practice. It was intended to avoid suspicion arising and prevent unfounded charges from being made. However, if a presbyter really has committed some fault and his guilt is proved beyond doubt by two or three witnesses (5:9), he must be taken to task publicly and rebuked mercilessly. It is not clear whether publicly means in the presence of all the presbyters or of the whole community. Such disciplinary measures should have a salutary influence and inspire the other presbyters with a fear of sin.

This rule seems so important to Paul that he solemnly adjures his representative to follow his instructions. In words which are weighted with gravity and solemnity, he warns Timothy to fulfill this duty with complete impartiality, to the exclusion of all personal preferences for or against the accused. This he must do in view of Christ's future coming and the final judgment which will take place in the sight of the whole court of heaven which consists of God, Jesus Christ, and the angels who are chosen. Paul is aware that the preservation of discipline will be doubly difficult if Timothy who is so young (4:12) is forced to take steps against an older man who is a leader of the community. However, where a fault or a sin has been committed, no human consideration or disinclination should prevent the proper sentence being passed or a penalty being imposed. Otherwise, discipline in the community will collapse completely.

22*Do not lay hands on anyone prematurely, or incur a share of the responsibility for the sins of another. Keep yourself free from stain.*

In his anxiety to ensure that only worthy presbyters will be appointed to rule the community, Paul warns his representative not to lay hands on anyone prematurely or entrust him with an office in the church. An overhasty choice which has not been sufficiently examined, and the appointment to office of an unworthy person which results from it, would make Timothy responsible, to some extent, for all the sins committed by such a person. Timothy's responsibility is a heavy one. The slightest negligence in the choice of presbyters may make him responsible for the sins of others. If he is to be able to arrive at a sound judgment concerning such persons, he must keep himself "free from stain." He must be an example to everyone by reason of the blameless, upright, and irreproachable character of his life.

23 *Do not be content to drink only water any more. Take a little wine for the good of your stomach and your frequent attacks of weakness.*

Without the slightest reference to the context or any form of introduction, Paul here gives his disciple some advice concerning his health. Because of his weak state of health, he must not drink "only water" in future; he must also take a little wine. We are not told why Timothy had previously confined himself to water. It is scarcely likely that the reason for such asceticism was in any way connected with the condemned views professed by the heretics. This piece of advice shows us how much Paul cared for his "son in the faith" and his well-being. The remark confirms the picture of the Apostle as a man with a heart full of goodness and loving care.

24 *In the case of many people, their sins are clearly visible and*

anticipate investigation. In the case of others, they come to light only after investigation. [25]*In the same way, good works are also clearly visible; if they are not, they cannot continue to be hidden.*

It seems that these remarks are intended to give the reason for the *discretion* necessary in choosing someone for office in the church. It is Paul's wish that only those be admitted to leadership of the community whose lives are firmly rooted in the faith. They must be of good character morally and be able to stand the test of the most searching examination. That is why he implies that no further investigation is necessary in the case of men whose behavior is clearly good or bad, to see whether they are worthy or not. However, there are secret, hidden sins which only come to light after a careful and penetrating scrutiny, just as a person's good deeds may also be completely hidden. In such cases, a conscientious and rigorous investigation is necessary and it is strictly obligatory. This will make possible a clear decision concerning such a person's moral worth or his lack of it and his fitness for the office.

Slaves (6:1–2)

Paul concludes his directions to Timothy for the proper discharge of his duties with a few brief words devoted to slaves. Together with widows (5:3–16), they are the poorest Christians in the church. It is significant that Paul gives his representative special instructions concerning them. We know from the writings of the New Testament that solicitude for the numerous slaves in the church occupied an important place in the life of the early Christian communities.

[1]*All those who are subject to the yoke as slaves must regard*

their masters as deserving all respect, so that God's name and the Christian teaching may not be badly spoken of.

Paul was very familiar with the desperate plight of slaves. He describes their life as one of "subjection to the yoke." Beasts of burden which are harnessed to the yoke are weighed down by its weight and forced to carry it. In the same way, these human beings are oppressed by their status as slaves; they are deprived of their freedom and forced to carry the heavy burden of their lives. They are constantly at the disposal of their masters and are not free to decide for themselves. This presents slaves who are Christians with a particularly serious problem. If his master is a *pagan,* a Christian slave must not become aggressive in his relations with him, even though he is now Christ's freeman (1 Cor. 7:22) and is fully conscious of his sublime dignity as a Christian. He must not refuse to show him respect. Otherwise, the infant church might be seriously endangered, as Paul sees quite clearly. Pagans would speak contemptuously of God and of the teachings of Christianity. They would blame the Christian faith for making their slaves insolent and speak badly about it. It was inevitable that pagans should judge Christianity on the evidence of the lives Christians led. Christian slaves, therefore, were bound to present a favorable image of the gospel of Christ by their respectful attitude and their sincere and conscientious devotion to duty. A genuinely Christian life is the best possible apology for Christianity. Such a life is based on a true and firm faith and is dedicated to the service of others in a sincere spirit of devotion to duty.

2*Those who have masters who are Christians must not think less of them because they are brethren. On the contrary, they* *should work all the more eagerly because they are Christians and beloved (brethren) who devote themselves to good works. Teach them this and bring it home to them.*

Paul turns his thoughts here to a different situation; a Christian slave's master may himself be a *Christian*. In this case, the equality of master and slave before God must not cause the slave to think less of his master. He must not confuse equality on a religious plane with equality on a social level. Even though in the eyes of God he is on a level with his Christian master as his brother, this of itself does not immediately abolish all social distinctions. Rather, he is bound to be doubly enthusiastic about his work. Slave and master are brothers in Christ and God's love extends to both alike. Of course, a master who is a Christian has special obligations to his Christian slave; he must show his brotherly love for him by his deeds. In complete harmony with other passages of the New Testament, Paul here does not abrogate the existing legal norms governing the relationship between slaves and their masters. For the moment, he makes no effort to introduce social changes. However, by proclaiming the Christian faith and the need for genuine love, he prepared the way from within for a reappraisal of the whole structure of society which was bound to lead to the abolition of slavery eventually. Where the Christian faith is really lived and Christian love prevails, the freedom of the individual is assured. There men are released from slavery.

FURTHER REFERENCES TO THE HERETICS (6:3–19)

In the concluding section of his letter, Paul once more issues a warning against the evil ways of the heretics (6:3–10). He calls upon Timothy to stand firm in the faith, while leading a life of blameless character and loyal service (6:11–16). In conclusion, he repeats his warning to the rich to make good use of their wealth (6:17–19).

The Pride and Greed of the Heretics (6:3–10)

3*If someone teaches false doctrines and does not hold fast to the sound words of our Lord Jesus Christ and the doctrine which is in keeping with holiness . . .*

The deepest reason why these people withdraw from the community and separate themselves from it lies in the fact that they do not hold fast to " the sound words " of our Lord Jesus Christ. They have abandoned the revelation which comes from God. Only such doctrine is " sound "; it is free from the germs of religious or moral illness and can keep a man in good spiritual health. The heretics have also abandoned the " doctrine which is in keeping with holiness "; they have rejected the teaching of the church. Paul deliberately refers to the teaching of the church and the Lord's words in one breath. The teaching of the church is the Lord's teaching; now that he has been raised to glory,

Christ will remain with his church uninterruptedly until the end of the world (Mt. 28:20). He sent her the Holy Spirit, to teach her everything, and recall all that he had said (Jn. 14:26). Rejection of Christ's teaching, just like rejection of the church's teaching, leads inevitably to heresy and error. Only unshakable faith in Christ's message as it is preached by the church and loyal attachment to him can preserve Christians from such errors and false paths.

[4a]*. . . he is blind and understands nothing. He is suffering from an excess of subtlety and controversies about words . . .*

Such apostasy from Christ's revelation and the teaching of the Church is not based on deeper insight into revealed truth. It is the result of presumption, conceitedness, and vain imagination. The efforts of the heretics to shine by reason of their subtleties and hair-splitting are a sign of their interior corruption and spiritual illness. Heretics in all ages have always appealed to the deeper insight and the fuller knowledge they enjoyed. However, there is no human insight, no human wisdom which can surpass Jesus' words or the church's teaching. Jesus' words and the church's teaching are the only source of divine truth.

[4b]*. . . which only give rise to jealousy and disputes, invective and unfounded suspicions.* [5]*This attitude is a source of constant discord among men whose intellects are corrupt and deprived of the truth. They think sanctity is a means of earning a living.*

The regrettable results which follow are in keeping with their pride and conceit. These are the evil fruits which seeds like these are bound to produce in such soil. The brotherly love which should be characteristic of Christians is destroyed and the community is split into different factions. Those who have proved themselves more eloquent or gifted in disputing about words arouse the jealousy of others because they are held in higher esteem by the common people. Fuel is constantly added to the flames by renewed hair-splitting. Where arguments based on reason no longer exist, people have recourse to invective and innuendo. Constant discord and unrest spread rapidly; the love which " does not claim its due, but believes all things, hopes all things, endures all things " (see 1 Cor. 13:5–7), which should be shared by the whole community, is destroyed. This is the work of individuals whose intellects have been dulled by their excessive self-esteem and their pride.

Such an attitude inevitably leads to the rejection of God's eternal truth. Paul refers with particular emphasis to the fact that the heretics regard their sanctity as a " means of making a living." They put it to bad use and regard religion as a form of business. It is probable that they insisted on being paid dearly for the alleged deeper insights which they offered their hearers in the course of meetings or instructions which they held. In this way, they exploited their followers. They may also have availed of the great numbers who flocked to the meetings and the deep impression their pious behavior and their preaching created, to enrich themselves.

[6]*In reality, holiness is a means to a rich reward, when it is accompanied by contentment.* [7]*We brought nothing with us into the world, and we can bring nothing out with us.* [8]*If we have food and clothing, we are readily content with that.*

To their perverse conduct Paul now contrasts the Christian

viewpoint. He had already explained before, "Holiness is useful in all circumstances, because it carries with it a promise for this life and for the next" (4:8). It possesses "life" here in this world, that true, eternal life which exists here on earth, the fullness of which is promised only for the life to come. True holiness, therefore, is the source of a great reward both for time and eternity. However, it must be accompanied by Christian contentment. It must be free from all greed for money and content with the gift God has bestowed.

In his efforts to give his readers a true idea and a proper esteem of the value of earthly possessions, Paul uses a thought which was already expressed in the Old Testament and in other passages of the New Testament.

It was also a commonplace of contemporary philosophy. We human beings enter the world naked and destitute; and we must leave it in the same state. Of all that we have owned here, we can take nothing with us. Earthly possessions are important only for the short duration of our life on earth. A man is sufficiently well off, therefore, if he has enough to feed and clothe himself. If he amasses a fortune and seeks security in it, God will say to him, "You fool! This very night your life will be demanded of you. And all the wealth you have amassed, whose shall it be now?" (Lk. 12:20).

[9]*Those who are anxious to become rich fall into temptation and various snares, the many foolish and shameful lusts which thrust men into ruin and perdition.* [10]*Indeed, avarice is the root of all evil; that is why many who strove to become rich strayed from the faith and prepared for themselves innumerable and excruciating torments.*

From his varied experience, Paul was only too well acquainted with the passion for wealth. That is why he condemns those who are possessed by a passionate lust for wealth and give themselves up to it completely. Such eagerness to amass wealth and build up a fortune, which is really a form of hunger for gold, has terrible consequences, and in the end it will hurl a man into eternal perdition. Greed such as this makes a man capable of anything. It degrades him and makes him a slave of lusts which reach passionate intensity. It leads to the ruin of his soul in time and in eternity. Paul must have known from experience that many Christians who were enslaved to the world by their greed had been estranged from Christ and had fallen away from the faith. They now suffer terrifying qualms of conscience because of their worldly wealth. For a Christian, however, there is only one choice and it is clear: "You cannot serve God and wealth" (Mt. 6:24). Avarice, therefore, is incompatible with the Christian faith and Christian sanctity.

An Appeal to Timothy to Fight the Good Fight (6:11–16)

11*For your part, you must flee all this, as a man of God. The aim of your striving must be justice, holiness, faith, love, endurance, and gentleness.*

Paul addresses Timothy as a "man of God." As a Christian, he is God's servant and he is on God's side. However, the expression implies more than this; he is a "man of God" because, like the prophets in the Old Testament, he has a particularly close and intimate relationship with God. By choice and by profession, he has consecrated his whole life to him. He cannot serve two masters; therefore, he must flee avarice, the great vice of this world. Like a person who is running in a different race, he must set his heart on a different goal, the virtues which govern his relationship with God (" holiness ") and his fellow men (" justice "). In addition, he must aim at the basic Christian values, faith, love, endurance, and the gentleness which bears with the sins and faults of one's brothers, in a spirit of forgiving love. The goal Timothy must reach, therefore, is the perfection of his interior life which involves all the human and Christian virtues.

12*Fight the good fight of faith; lay your grasp on the eternal life to which you have been called, for which you bore courageous testimony before so many witnesses.*

A truly Christian life is a glorious *contest* in which the competitors are animated by faith. The prize is eternal life. God himself had invited Timothy to take part in it and Timothy had responded to this call by bearing courageous testimony before a great number of witnesses. It is impossible to say when exactly he bore this witness. It is probable that it was on the day he received baptism. From the earliest times it was customary to make a solemn profession of faith on that day, in which the newly baptized Christian asserted his belief in eternal life. It may also have been the day of his ordination and installation in office as a presbyter that Timothy made a public profession of his faith in the teaching of Christ. Every Christian is entered for this contest, just like Timothy; every Christian is called to this by God; and every Christian must answer God's call by professing his faith.

[13]*I command you before God who gives life to all things and before Christ Jesus who bore glorious witness under Pontius Pilate:* [14]*Keep the commandment without fail and without stain until the coming of our Lord Jesus Christ . . .*

Paul once more addresses his representative in a manner which is particularly solemn; it almost resembles a formal injunction under oath. He calls upon God as his witness, the Lord who is our creator and redeemer, the source of all natural and supernatural life, and upon Jesus Christ. By his passion and his sacrifice of himself in his death on the cross under Pontius Pilate, Christ bore glorious witness to his claim to be the Messiah and God's Son. By his blameless and holy life, Timothy must "keep the commandment," the Christian faith in its entirety, until Jesus Christ comes to pass judgment on the world. Christ's second coming is described as an "epiphany," that is, a sudden visit from a king and one which is close at hand. Then Jesus will leave his place of concealment and appear before the whole world and so reveal his eternal kingdom. Paul had one great wish and he is anxious to bring it home to his representative as emphatically as possible. This is the preservation of the Christian faith, pure and unadulterated, in the face of all the attacks of the heretics, until the last day. The first and most important task confronting any Christian is the preservation of his faith by living a good life, despite the dangers which surround him.

[15]*. . . which he, the blessed One who alone is Lord, will reveal in due time. He is king of kings and lord of lords.* [16]*He alone possesses immortality; he lives in unapproachable light which no human being has seen or can see. To him belong honor and dominion. Amen.*

We human beings have no idea *when* the " coming of our Lord Jesus Christ " will take place. God alone knows the moment, the " due time," when it will happen. It is for us Christians to await it in constant readiness.

Paul's admonition culminates in wonderfully fervent prayer, a hymn of praise to God. By his omnipotence and his universal dominion, God is raised far above everything mortal. The power of earthly lords or kings is as nothing in his sight. Despite their deification in the emperor-worship of the time, they are all mortal. God alone, in the fullness of his being, possesses immortality and lives in unapproachable light. No human intellect can attain knowledge of him or draw near him, unless he himself elevates it by his grace and gives it light. The prayer concludes with an expression of praise in which God's infinite and eternal power is underlined. In this passage as in so many others in his letters, Paul's mind comes to rest only *in adoring God*. His heart is ever restless, until it finds its rest in God.

The Correct Use of Wealth (6:17–19)

We should have expected that our letter would end with this hymn of praise to God (6:15f.). However, Paul adds a postscript in which he gives Timothy some instructions for the wealthy members of his community.

17*Impress upon those who are rich in this world that they must not grow haughty. They must set their hope, not in their wealth which may fail them, but in God who gives us so plentifully everything we enjoy.*

Paul has already warned against the passionate pursuit of wealth (6:9f.). He now gives a number of directions for the wealthy members of the community entrusted to Timothy's pastoral care on the use to which they should put their wealth. Even if a person has acquired his wealth perfectly honestly, it may still be full of danger for him. Paul warns such people against setting their hopes in their "wealth which may fail them"; he calls on them, instead, to place all their trust in God. Wealth and possessions are of use only in this world. They perish and are snatched away from a man without warning, as Jesus explained so clearly in the parable of the rich man (Lk. 12:16–21). Pride, presumptuousness, and false reliance on the power of wealth and possessions which is so uncertain, are dangers which threaten all men. A Christian must set all his hope and trust in God's fatherly goodness. In his love, God will give his children all they need. Our Lord's own advice in the Sermon on the Mount is meant for them: "Do not worry about your life, what you are to eat or what you are to drink; and do not worry about your body, how you are to clothe it . . . Pagans spend themselves in pursuit of such things. Your heavenly Father knows that you need them all" (Mt. 6:25, 32).

18*They should do good and grow rich in charitable deeds; they must be generous and ready to give;* 19*in this way, they will lay a firm foundation for themselves for the future, so as to attain true life.*

In these verses Paul warns us against another danger inherent in wealth. A wealthy person must not shut his heart selfishly against the needs of his fellow men. On the contrary, he must fulfill the Christian obligation of love by his actions. Real wealth for a Christian should consist in being rich in good deeds. Anyone who follows Paul's instructions will lay a " good foundation " for himself by his active love; he will have an invisible treasure in heaven. He contributes to his own entrance into eternal life, which is the only " true " life. This is the way a Christian becomes rich " in God's eyes " (Lk. 12:21); he " stores up treasure in heaven " (Mk. 6:20) and the Father " who sees what is hidden will reward him for it " (Mt. 6:4). Of course, he must always remember that " true life," eternal salvation, is a pure gift of God's grace, which no human being can merit for himself. All the works of charity he performs are ultimately God's works; it was he who poured his own love into the Christian's heart.

THE CLOSE OF THE LETTER
(6:20-21)

CONCLUSION (6:20–21)

A Final Warning Against Heretics (6:20–21a)

[20]Timothy, keep safe what has been entrusted to you. Avoid profane, empty talk, and the controversies which spring from what is called knowledge but is false. [21a]Some people who professed to have such knowledge have strayed from the faith.

In these two concluding verses Paul once more sums up the two most important themes of his letter: the *preservation* of the Christian faith and the energetic *repudiation* of heresy. Paul had entrusted his representative with the Christian faith as with a priceless treasure which had to be kept safely. Keeping it pure and unadulterated is Timothy's most important task; it is his duty as an office-bearer in the community. It is for him to hand on this precious legacy. The deposit with which Timothy has been "entrusted" includes the whole teaching of the Christian faith which must be the norm of a genuinely Christian way of life. To preserve the deposit of faith and keep it safe, Timothy must "avoid" heresy. He must simply reject it, without arguing too much with the heretics. Their doctrines are merely "profane, empty talk." They appeal to new "knowledge," which does not really deserve this name because it contradicts the only true knowledge revealed by God. With its pretense of profundity, this "occult science" hopes to give people fresh knowledge of God and the world. However, it abandons the sure ground of the faith and lapses into error. His own experience enables Paul to point to the evil consequences of such heretical doctrines. Some of the community have already become devotees of this " talk " and abandoned their faith in Christ. This is a serious warning to Timothy and the whole community.

Good Wishes (6:21b)

21b *Grace be with you.*

This final good wish is intended for Timothy and the whole community; in dealing with the different points raised in his letter, Paul had them constantly in mind. Paul sends them the best wish one Christian can send another, " grace." This is God's grace by which we are saved and which will be revealed in all its glory in " the world to come."

The Second Epistle
To Timothy

INTRODUCTION

We have already seen that in 1 Timothy Paul was mainly concerned with outlining the tasks which his representative would have to face in Macedonia. These included the struggle against heretics within the Christian community, and the preservation of the life and organization of the church. After his arrest, St. Paul once more wrote to his disciple from his prison in Rome. With an insistence peculiar to a last message, he solemnly calls on him to fulfill his office conscientiously and to profess the faith loyally. He also gives him instructions on how to deal with heretics, and describes his personal circumstances.

1. Paul found himself in close custody in Rome, so that he was condemned to inactivity and could do nothing to further the spread of the gospel. He knew, on the one hand, that heretics were threatening the churches he had founded; on the other hand, he also knew his death was near. That is why he makes a *personal appeal* to Timothy, his beloved son (1:2), with all the earnestness and insistence of a final message. He calls on him to fan the flame of the grace God gave him, which dwells in him as a result of the imposition of his hands (1:6). He must never lose heart, despite all his labors in preaching the gospel. The spirit God gave him was not a spirit of fear; it was a spirit of strength, of love, and of discipline (1:7). Consequently, he must never be ashamed of the witness he bears to our Lord Jesus Christ; nor must he be ashamed of Paul, even though the latter is now in prison and laden with chains like a criminal (1:8, 16f.; 2:9). He must profess his faith fearlessly and plead the cause of the gospel

with the strength which comes from God (1:8). He must be strong in the grace which has its source in Jesus Christ (2:1). In contrast to the heretics and the fantasies they indulge in, he must keep a sober mind (4:5). He must devote himself to preaching the gospel and proclaim the good news everywhere (4:5). In this way, he will always do his duty to the full (4:5).

As a Christian, and especially as an office-bearer in the community and as Paul's representative, Timothy is really a soldier of Jesus Christ. Consequently, he must be prepared to suffer with Christ (2:3), and share Paul's readiness to endure hardship. In union with him, he must suffer for the gospel and expose himself to persecution and insults, in the strength which comes from God (1:8). As the soldier of a commander-in-chief who lives in heaven, it is his duty to spend himself without reserve in his service and in the service of the message he brings (2:4). He must never allow himself to be distracted from this duty by the business of daily life. Otherwise, he will bring upon himself the displeasure of his commanding officer (2:4). Like an athlete entered for a contest, he must abide by the rules, or run the risk of missing the prize (2:5). If he wants to have the first share in the harvest, he must work like a farm-laborer, in the sweat of his brow (2:6). That is why he must shun the ardors of youth (2:22) and make justice, faith, and love the goal of all his striving (2:22). He must be friendly towards everyone and not be given to quarreling (2:24). At the same time, he must not be surprised if he has to suffer persecution. This is the lot of every Christian who wishes to live a good life in Jesus Christ (3:12). Paul warns Timothy especially against Alexander the coppersmith. He had been a great opponent of his preaching and had done him a lot of harm (4:14).

Paul himself should serve as Timothy's model in preaching

the sound doctrine of the gospel. He must hold fast, in faith and love, to what he has heard from him (1:13). In point of fact, Timothy had already adopted Paul's teaching, his way of life, and his readiness to endure suffering as his model (3:10ff.). By the power of the Holy Spirit who dwells in him, he must preserve the integrity of the gospel, the revealed truth with which he was entrusted (1:14). He must keep Jesus Christ firmly before his mind's eye, Jesus who comes from the tribe of David, whom God raised from the dead after his death on the cross (2:8). He has proved his worth as a workman in God's eyes and now he must proclaim the truth ever more clearly (2:15).

Timothy has one other special obligation; he must find reliable persons to whom he can entrust the gospel, men who will be able to teach it to others, in their turn (2:2). So he will ensure that God's word is handed down to future generations in all its purity. He must hold fast by the faith; he knows from whom he received it, and he is well versed in the sacred scripture of the Old Testament from his childhood (3:14). Only by so doing will he be equal to all the demands of his calling and prepared for every noble task (3:17). In the sight of God and Jesus Christ, the Judge who is to come, Paul solemnly appeals to his disciple and reminds him of his duty to preach God's word, no matter whether it is welcome or unwelcome to those who hear it (4:1f.). The reason for this solemn appeal lies in the fact that heretics had made their appearance and constituted a threat to the church (4:3).

2. The *danger* which these heretics represented to the community moved Paul to give his representative directions on how to deal with them. They were already active in the church and their false teachings spread like a cancer which consumed all before it (2:17). Every day they sank further into a state of god-

lessness (2 : 16). Paul mentions two of them by name, Hymenaeus and Philetas, who were probably leaders among them (2 : 17). He had already told Timothy in his first letter that he had expelled Hymenaeus from the church (1 Tim. 1 : 20). Both men had strayed from the revealed truth, and taught that the resurrection had already taken place (2 : 18). Their activities made them a danger to the faith and, in the case of some Christians, they had already destroyed it (2 : 18).

The heretics were evil men and impostors, and they continued on their way from bad to worse. They had gone astray themselves and they led others astray with them (3 : 13). They were ensnared by the wiles of the devil and completely at his disposal (2 : 26). The reason for their false teaching was that they had abandoned the truth and turned to fables (4 : 4). Indeed, they set themselves up in opposition to the truth. In former times, Jannes and Jambres, Moses' great opponents, had resisted him. In the same way, the heretics resisted the truth; their minds were perverted and they were completely untried in the faith (3 : 8).

That was why they found the truth which had been revealed, the " sound doctrine " of the gospel, unbearable. They shook it off, as if it were a heavy burden, and sought out teachers to suit themselves. They rejected the teachers appointed by the church, because they were only interested in what appealed to their own ears and soothed them with flattery (4 : 3). They made their way furtively from house to house and were constantly on the lookout for new disciples in the community (3 : 6). In this way, they won over women who had a bad name and were burdened with sins (3 : 6), because they allowed themselves to be guided by their lusts and passions (3 : 6). The heretics pretended to be willing to learn and to be always in search of the truth. Yet they never arrived at genuine faith or recognition of the truth (3 : 7).

Despite the threat to the church which the heretics represented, Timothy must never lose heart or become discouraged. These false teachers will make no further gains because their folly will be apparent to all (3:9). Moreover, the church which God has established so firmly will remain unshaken (2:19). No matter how fanatically the heretics struggle against the truth of the gospel, the church will stand firm. The fate of Christians is in God's hands; they are safe in his love. He knows them and he will protect them in his love. The appearance of the heretics and their activities should not even surprise Timothy, or lead Christians astray in their faith. A large household contains utensils of the most varied kinds; they are made of different materials and used for a variety of purposes. In the same way, Christians may be destined for the most varied types of service in the church, which is God's household (2:20). Unfortunately, even in the church there are Christians who have fallen into error and dishonor the church; they are susceptible to the false doctrines of the heretics. However, they are not lost yet. It is within their power to purify themselves of their faults and become useful members of the community once more (2:21).

How is Timothy to deal with these heretics? He must not allow himself to be drawn into controversy with them or engage in wordy disputes (2:14). Such an approach would be fruitless; it would only make things worse (2:15). Instead, he should proclaim the truth, God's revelation in the gospel, without deviating from the right path (2:15). Moreover, he should avoid the profane, meaningless talk of these false teachers. He must simply reject their silly, foolish chatter; he should know well that discussion is no use; it will only make matters worse (2:23). As a "servant of the Lord," he is expected to be above such disputes (2:24).

Timothy's whole approach should be to let others see something of the goodness and love of his heart. Therefore, he must be friendly towards everyone (2:24). He must remain calm and show inexhaustible patience to all. He must make known the gospel teaching in the most suitable way possible and gently reprove those who oppose it (2:25). If Timothy gives proof of genuine, patient, and self-sacrificing love in this way, perhaps God will grant those who have been led astray a change of heart, and bring them back once more to knowledge of the truth and the true faith (2:25). Timothy should keep away from the heretics and not have any closer contact with them than this (3:5). The moral decay which is characteristic of the last stage of time and has been predicted for the " last days," is already evident in them. This is the wickedness and corruption which is described in a frightening picture in 3:1–4.

3. In this letter Paul gives his correspondent more detailed information concerning his *personal circumstances* at the time of writing than in either 1 Timothy or the Epistle to Titus. The letter comes from a prison in Rome (1:8, 16f.; 2:9), where the Apostle is treated like a criminal (2:8). The reason for his imprisonment is that he preached the good news of Jesus Christ who came from the tribe of David, whom God raised from the dead, after his death on the cross (2:9). Paul is not ashamed of his fetters (1:12), because the gospel is the cause of his detention; his conscience is clear (1:3). He is happy to have to endure the sufferings which accompany his imprisonment. He bears it all patiently and willingly for the sake of the " elect," that they may attain salvation and eternal glory (3:10).

Although his captivity has reduced him to enforced idleness, Paul is conscious that the " message " of the gospel remains unfettered (2:9). Even in prison he is still the herald, the apostle, and the teacher of the gospel (1:11). He is absolutely convinced that God has the power to keep the gospel message safe (1:12) and ensure that it will not be corrupted, despite his imprisonment. He is so possessed by his calling as an apostle that he refers to his first appearance before the tribunal as an opportunity to proclaim the gospel. He firmly believes that, in this way, he is fulfilling the task God gave him by making him the Apostle of the gentiles (4:17). Even in prison he is still occupied with the care of his churches. That is why he sends Tychicus to Ephesus (4:12) and is anxious that Mark should come to Rome, where he can put his " services " to good use, for the benefit of the gospel (4:11).

Paul's intimate friendship with his disciple Timothy is movingly revealed in this letter. He remembers him constantly, day and night, in his prayers (1:3), and recalls their sad parting (1:4). He acknowledges the genuine faith which his disciple (1:5) shared with his mother Eunice and his grandmother Lois (1:5). In the loneliness of his captivity, therefore, which was shared only by his faithful fellow worker Luke (4:11), it was quite understandable that he should have longed with all his heart to see Timothy once more (1:4). This would give him great joy (1:4). In three different passages, he asks Timothy to come to him at any cost (4:9, 13, 21), and to come quickly, so that the winter which prevented traveling by sea and the sentence of death which must soon come, might not make a reunion impossible (4:21).

He tells his trusted follower about the others who shared his work. Demas had abandoned him, through love for the world, and gone to Thessalonica, while Crescens had left for Galatia and Titus for Dalmatia (4:10). He also tells him about the places he visited on his last journey before his arrest; Troas, where he left his mantle behind with Carpus (4:13); Corinth, where Erastus remained behind, and Miletus, where he was forced to leave Trophimus because he was ill (4:20). He gives him one last command, to bring Mark with him to Rome; he can make good use of him (4:11). Finally, Paul makes known his last wish, that Timothy would bring with him the mantle which he had left with Carpus and his books, especially the rolls of parchment (4:13).

Paul had experienced great joy and deep sorrow in his imprisonment. It was a cause of joy to him that Onesiphorus, on his arrival in Rome, should have sought him out so eagerly and refused to be ashamed of him, while encouraging him with his frequent visits (1:16–18). On the other hand, he felt great sorrow that all the Christians from Asia should have abandoned him and left him in the lurch. Among these were Phigellus and Hermogenes; these must have been fellow workers of his, from whom he might have expected more. Alexander the coppersmith had caused him great suffering; he had done him a lot of harm and opposed his message bitterly (4:14). His greatest disappointment, however, and his sharpest pain, came at the moment of his first appearance in court. His burning sorrow is movingly expressed in the brief statement, "They all left me in the lurch" (4:16). However, God did not abandon him, even though his friends had failed him; he gave him courage and rescued him from the "lion's jaws" (4:17). Paul's stature is enhanced all the more by this incident; he was not bowed down or crushed by the opposition of his enemies, or the cowardice and disloyalty of his friends.

When Paul wrote this letter to Timothy, he knew that his death must come without delay. His first defense had been successful (4:16f.), but he no longer had hopes of an acquittal and expected to be condemned to death. He is well prepared to die. He accepts the death which faces him with full consciousness and without flinching; he offers himself up as a sacrificial victim, knowing that this is the way to union with God (4:6). In perfect peace and calm, he can look back over a life filled with suffering and persecution, from which God had always saved him (3:11).

In his rich, full life, he had fought the good fight and kept faith with God (4:7). In his deep faith and unshakable hope, he had every reason to look forward to the crown of victory (4:8) and entrance into the heavenly kingdom (4:18). Undaunted by opposition or suffering, Paul goes to his death full of courage and strength. In this letter he gives Timothy his last will and testament.

OUTLINE

The Opening of the Letter (1:1–2)

INTRODUCTORY VERSES

I. The sender and the addressee (1:1–2a)

II. Greetings (1:2b)

The Body of the Letter (1:3—4:8)

AN APPEAL FOR FIDELITY IN THE SERVICE OF THE GOSPEL (1:3—2:13)

I. Thanksgiving for Timothy's loyalty to the faith and longing for reunion (1:3–5)
   1. Thanksgiving (1:3)
   2. Longing for reunion (1:4–5)

II. Paul appeals to Timothy to profess his faith courageously and be willing to suffer (1:6–14)
   1. Keep safe the gift of grace and bear frank witness to the Lord (1:6–8a)
   2. Readiness to suffer through God's power (1:8b–12)
   3. Hold fast to the teaching handed down (1:13–14)

III. Paul's bitter disappointment; Onesiphorus is praised for his loyalty (1:15–18)
   1. His bitter experiences in Asia (1:15)
   2. Onesiphorus' loyalty (1:16–18)

IV. Paul calls on Timothy to hand on the tradition received from the apostles and exhorts him once more to be willing to suffer (2:1–13)

1. The transmission of what has been received from the apostle to men who could be trusted (2:1–2)
2. An appeal for readiness to suffer as Christ's soldier (2:3–7)
3. Jesus' resurrection (2:8–13)

THE PROPER ATTITUDE TOWARDS HERETICS (2:14—4:8)

I. A warning against useless disputes and empty talk (2:14–21)
   1. A warning against disputes (2:14–15)
   2. A warning against empty talk (2:16–18)
   3. God's firm foundation (2:16–18)

II. Paul appeals to Timothy to lead an exemplary Christian life and instruct those who have strayed in a spirit of charity (2:22–26)
   1. An appeal for a genuinely Christian life (2:22–23)
   2. Instruct those who have strayed in a spirit of charity (2:24–26)

III. The activities of the heretics as the beginning of the final corruption to come (3:1–9)
   1. Paul foretells the moral degeneracy to come at the end of time (3:1–5)
   2. The activities of the heretics as the beginning of this corruption (3:6–9)

IV. An appeal for loyalty and steadfastness (3:10–17)
   1. Paul appeals to Timothy to remain faithful to the example of his life and teaching (3:10–13)
   2. An exhortation to hold fast to sacred scripture (3:14–17)

V. Unwearied service of the truth (4:1–8)
   1. Paul makes an urgent appeal to Timothy to preach God's word (4:1–4)
   2. Wholehearted devotion to the service of the truth (4:5–8)

The Close of the Letter (4:9–22)

CONCLUSION (4:9–22)

I. News about Paul's fellow missionaries (4:9–12)
II. Paul makes a request of Timothy (4:13)
III. A warning against Alexander the coppersmith (4:14–15)
IV. The gravity of Paul's situation (4:16–18)
V. Greetings (4:19–21)
VI. Good wishes (4:22)

THE OPENING OF THE LETTER
(1:1-2)

INTRODUCTORY VERSES (1:1–2)

The Sender and the Addressee (1:1–2a)

[1]Paul, by God's will an apostle of Jesus Christ for the life promised in Christ, [2]to Timothy, his beloved son . . .

Although the letter is addressed to Timothy, his "beloved son," who had been his fellow worker and his disciple for years, the inscription lays great stress on the writer's authority. He is an *apostle,* an accredited representative of Jesus Christ. We must remember the letter is not merely a private letter, intended for Timothy alone. It is an official communication from the Apostle. It is true that it is intended primarily—and to a greater extent than 1 Timothy—for Timothy personally, but it is also addressed to the community in which Timothy was his representative.

Paul is an apostle, not by his own choice or on his own initiative, but by "God's will." It was God who chose him and called him to be his authorized spokesman, and he fitted him for his task. In virtue of this authority, Paul takes up his pen and writes this letter to his disciple and to the church, so that what he writes has official standing. Behind the Apostle of the gentiles, with all his authority, stands Jesus Christ himself, and ultimately God. It is from God that this message comes to Timothy and the church. Not only are the readers bound to take notice of what the letter says; they also owe it obedience.

The aim and purpose of the mission which the author has received as an apostle is to make known the *life* which God has *promised*. This is that eternal life which is rooted in communion of faith and life with Jesus Christ. It survives physical death and conquers it, reaching its full development only after the resurrection. Paul realized that his death was at hand. His life was coming to an end (see 4:6–8), and it was precisely at this moment that the thought and the certainty of the eternal life he enjoyed in Christ Jesus overwhelmed him (see 1 Tim. 4:8). The certainty of eternal life which is assured us in Christ Jesus forms a solid foundation for the life of any Christian, in contrast to those who have "no hope" (1 Thess. 4:13).

The recipient of the letter is Timothy, his beloved son. Timothy was the son of a pagan father and a pious Jewish-Christian mother. He was probably converted to the Christian faith by Paul at Lystra on his first missionary journey. That is why he calls him "beloved and true son in the Lord" (1 Cor. 4:17), who "labored at the Lord's work," like Paul himself (1 Cor. 16:10), and cherished the same sentiments as his spiritual father. This is the praise that Paul gives him in the Epistle to the Philippians: "I have no one who shares my sentiment to the same extent, or is so genuinely concerned with your affairs . . . You know his well tried loyalty; together with me, he served the gospel, like a son helping his father" (2:20–22). Absolute reliability, devotedness, and unselfishness characterized this fellow worker of Paul's who had been with him for so many years and was united with him in fidelity and love.

Greetings (1:2b)

2b*Grace, mercy, and peace, from God the Father and Christ Jesus our Lord.*

Instead of the usual Greek or Jewish greeting (" Joy," " Peace "), Paul wishes his correspondent, *grace, mercy, and peace.* He raises the normal greeting in use at the time to a Christian level and wishes him all that seems most important in his eyes; " grace," the inexhaustible wealth of divine favour, which man can only receive, but never merit by his own efforts; " mercy," which is so necessary for sinful man, when we remember his complete dependence upon God and the distance between them; " peace," which we might better translate as " salvation." It includes man's eternal destiny, as well as everything else. Only God and Jesus Christ could be the source of such gifts. As God's Son and the risen Lord, Jesus is his equal and stands on the same level with him. This greeting is not meant to be an idle wish; it is intended to be effective, so that Timothy and the community will really receive the fullness of grace, mercy, and salvation. The fact that God is our " Father " and Jesus Christ is " our Lord " ensures this.

THE BODY OF THE LETTER
(1:3—4:8)

AN APPEAL FOR FIDELITY IN THE SERVICE OF THE GOSPEL (1:3—2:13)

The second letter to Timothy, like the first, is loosely put together. This is in contrast to Paul's other epistles, in which God's saving activity is described in the first part, to be followed in the second part by the consequences that this entails for the Christian life. Numerous appeals to Timothy to fulfill his office properly and instructions on how to deal with the heretics are loosely strung together with a description of Paul's situation in prison. In this letter, Paul is intent on encouraging his fellow missionary to proclaim God's word faithfully and he is also anxious to bolster his position as head of the church at Ephesus. That is why he gives him the support of his intervention as an apostle.

In the first part of the letter, therefore, Paul thanks God for Timothy's loyalty to the faith and expresses his longing to see him again (1:3–5). He calls on him to fan the flames of the gift of grace he had received and bear unflinching witness to his Lord. He must be prepared to suffer for the gospel, like Paul himself, and hold fast to the teaching which has been handed down (1:6–14). Paul himself had encountered many bitter experiences and disappointments on the part of the Christians from Asia. However, he had also met examples of great fidelity and had been comforted by the loyalty of Onesiphorus, which he emphasizes particularly (1:15–18). Strengthened by God's grace, Timothy in his turn must also hand on the teaching he had received from the Apostle in a way which could be depended upon. As a soldier of Jesus Christ, he must bear the sufferings and hardships his service entailed. The thought of the risen Lord should give him unshakable courage. Paul closes the first part of his letter with a prayer taken from an early Christian text (2:1–13).

Thanksgiving for Timothy's Loyalty to the Faith and Longing for Reunion (1:3–5)

Thanksgiving (1:3)

3 *I give thanks to the God whom I serve with a clear conscience, like my ancestors before me, as I remember you constantly in my prayers, day and night.*

In imitation of the ancient style of letter writing, Paul begins with an expression of thanks. However, he raises this convention to a Christian plane and offers his thanks to God. He sees *God's power* at work in the churches he had founded, as well as in the souls of all Christians and in his fellow worker Timothy. He knows that everything in his personal life, as in the life of the church, must be referred ultimately to God, from whom "every gift that is good and every perfect blessing comes" (Jas. 1:17). Everything must be an occasion for offering thanks, "so that such gratitude may overflow, to God's glory" (2 Cor. 4:15). That is why he tells the Christians at Thessalonica, "Give thanks for everything; that is God's will for you in Christ Jesus" (1 Thess. 5:18).

Paul offers thanks, as he remembers Timothy constantly in his prayers, *day and night*. He is his "beloved son" (1:2), "his own son in the faith" (1 Tim. 1:2), a "faithful son in the Lord" (1 Cor. 4:17). He was genuinely concerned for the welfare of the Christian community and had given proof of his fidelity by working in the service of the gospel, together with Paul (Phil. 2:20–22). Despite his youth (1 Tim. 4:12), he had been entrusted with the supervision of the church at Ephesus as the result of a prophecy (1 Tim. 1:18). There it was his task to defend the "sound doctrine" (1 Tim. 1:10; 6:3) contained in God's word against the heretics. Paul could never forget his fellow missionary or the work he had accomplished by the help of God's grace. That is why he never ceased to thank God.

He *serves God with a clear conscience,* like all his forefathers. Paul came from a pious Jewish family of the tribe of Benjamin. The God of his fathers is his God too, the one true God who made known his plan of salvation in the Old Testament as a promise, and brought it to its completion in the New Testament. This is the God that Paul served with a clear conscience, even before his conversion at Damascus (see Acts 24:14–16). After his arrest at Jerusalem, he could testify clearly and unambiguously before the Council, "Until the present day, I have lived before God's eyes with a good conscience" (Acts 23:1). In the presence of the Roman governor Felix, at Caesarea, he asserted that he had always done his best "to keep a clear conscience before God and men" (Acts 24:16).

On the other hand, had he not persecuted the church (Acts 26:9–11)? Had he not been a "blasphemer, a persecutor, and a criminal" (1 Tim. 1:13)? He had been, but it was the result of ignorance, unbelief (1 Tim. 1:13), and a mistaken zeal for God's glory (Acts 22:3; 26:9); it was not the result of human malice. Even yet, he served God with a clear conscience in his prison cell, although in the eyes of the world he seemed an ordinary criminal (2:9). It was solely because he proclaimed the gospel of Jesus Christ that he was in chains (2:9).

Despite the distance which separated them, therefore, Paul remained united in love with Timothy, his beloved son. In his hours of prayer and loneliness during his last imprisonment, he did not forget to intercede for his fellow missionary and his church. True prayer unites a Christian, not only with God, but also with his fellow Christians. It forms a bond of union between all those who are brothers and sisters in Christ.

Longing for Reunion (1:4-5)

4*I remember your tears and I long to see you, to be filled with*
joy. 5*Your sincere faith is fresh in my memory. It dwelt first in*
your grandmother Lois and your mother Eunice, but I am convinced that it lives in you too.

Paul recalls once more the sad and bitter moment when he said good-bye to Timothy. We do not know where or when this took place; it may have been at the time of his departure for Rome, where he was once more thrown into prison. In the loneliness of his cell he longs to see his disciple once more. He hopes that this will bring him unalloyed *joy*; in his present circumstances, such a visit could be a great *comfort* to him. This ardent yearning to see his fellow missionary pervades the whole letter. At the end, it wrings from him the fervent plea: Hurry and come to me (4:9, 21).

For the moment, however, Paul is forced to be content with the knowledge that his disciple is loyal to the faith. He finds comfort in this and in the thought that the pure faith which dwells in Timothy is God's gift. This *sincere faith*, this genuine and unreserved dedication of himself to his Lord and God in faith, is something which Timothy inherited from his family. His mother and his grandmother before him had set an example of true and unadulterated faith. It is probable that Paul had come to know both of them personally during his stay at Lystra (Acts 14:6, 8, 21; 16:1–3). These words clearly indicate what a blessing it is to come from a home where the parents have the faith and are truly religious. Paul makes no mention of Timothy's father; he had been a pagan (a Greek, see Acts 16:1) and was probably already dead.

Paul Appeals to Timothy to Profess His Faith Courageously and Be Willing to Suffer (1:6–14)

Keep Safe the Gift of Grace and Bear Frank Witness to the Lord (1:6–8a)

6 *For this reason I remind you: Enkindle God's gift of grace to new fervor, the grace which dwells in you as a result of the laying on of my hands.* 7 *It was not a spirit of fear God gave us; it was a spirit of strength and love and moderation.*

As head of the church at Ephesus, Timothy was in no easy position in the struggle against the heretics. Moreover, he was still young (see 1 Tim. 4:12) and of a rather timid disposition (see 1 Cor. 16:10f.). By his sincere faith and his undying love, he was united with Paul, and so Paul reminds him of *God's gift of grace* which dwells in him as the result of the imposition of his hands (1 Tim. 4:14). This gift was given to Timothy once and for all; it is his permanent possession and one he cannot lose.

In 1 Thessalonians 5:19, God's Spirit and the gift he brings are compared to a fire. So here the gift of grace Timothy received by the imposition of hands is similarly described. Like a fire, this gift may be nothing more than a glimmer, or it may light up and burn with all its strength, depending upon the living conviction with which it fills a person's consciousness. It gives Timothy all the strength he needs for his work; it remains with him in all the difficulties and struggles of his office, and it gives him joy and courage in the midst of his trials. Had Timothy become exhausted and discouraged, that Paul should remind him like this of the gift of grace he had received and appeal to him to kindle it to fresh fervor? As God's gift, it remained with him constantly. But it was up to him to ensure that it burned with all its ardor and became a source of strength in his ministry. He had to fan the flame by prayer and an attitude of genuine self-surrender.

As an office-bearer in the community, Timothy received, together with this gift of grace, *the spirit of strength and love and moderation.* These are the powers which accompany the supernatural life of grace. They serve to elevate man's natural powers and all his human virtualities. As they come from God, they are incompatible with fear or timidity in the face of the difficult task which confronts Timothy at Ephesus. This spirit is a divine power which will inspire him to labor effectively and minister unselfishly; it will be a source of strong, self-sacrificing love in the service of his brothers, and of self-control and prudent discretion in all his duties. In his goodness and condescension, God equips those who bear office with all the gifts they need to fulfill their difficult task.

8a*Do not be ashamed, therefore, of the witness you bear for our Lord, or of me, his prisoner.*

Strengthened with this divine power, Timothy will find the courage not to be ashamed of the witness he bears for our Lord;

he will not be afraid of professing his faith in him. The witness that Timothy bore our Lord was the message contained in God's word with which he had been entrusted. Those who welcomed this message and proclaimed it exposed themselves to insults and persecution. If he refuses to be ashamed of bearing witness to our Lord, Timothy will not be ashamed of Paul, " the Lord's prisoner," either. Paul's whole life was devoted to proclaiming the gospel; God had appointed him as a " herald " of the good news (1:11). Now, however, he was laden with chains like any ordinary criminal (2:9).

This appeal to Timothy reminds us of the words of our Lord, which were intended for all his followers: " If a man acknowledges me before men, I will acknowledge him before my Father in heaven " (Mt. 10:32).

Readiness to Suffer through God's Power (1:8b–12)

8b*Instead, you must suffer with me for the gospel, through God's power.*

Paul now goes a step further. It is not enough that Timothy should not be ashamed of him; he must also *suffer with him for the gospel, through God's power.* He must enter into a communion of suffering with Paul, as he had already done during his first imprisonment; he must come to Rome (4:9). In a world which was hostile to God, even the mere fact of bearing witness to Jesus of Nazareth who was crucified already involved serious risk. Paul's request, however, presupposed that Timothy was ready to make the supreme sacrifice, the sacrifice of his life. He himself was fully prepared to give his life. He realized clearly that his life was " already being offered up in sacrifice and that the time for his departure from this life had come " (4:6). In the same way, he demands that his representative should show a spirit of complete self-sacrifice in the service of the Lord and his gospel. Such devotedness, of course, and such self-sacrifice are possible for a human being only through God's power; they are beyond a man's strength. God's power, however, enables a man to endure any suffering and conquer it. Paul knew full well that he " could do all things in him who gave him strength " (Phil. 4:13). Timothy will experience the same divine favor.

[9]*He saved us and called us with a calling which is holy. It was not the result of any actions of ours; it was the result of his own decision, his own graciousness, the graciousness which he showed us in Christ Jesus before all ages.* [10]*Now it has been revealed because our Saviour, Christ Jesus, has appeared; he annihilated death and brought life and immortality to light through the gospel . . .*

The mention of the " gospel " reminds Paul of all God's saving activity in the history of salvation. In a few brief sentences which follow one another like the articles of a creed, he sums up the message of the gospel, all God's saving activity (see Tit. 3:4–7). The mystery of the redemption is expounded in three stages.

1. God revealed his intention of bringing mankind to salvation, as a result of which he has saved those who are Christians and sent his call to them. He is the *redeemer and saviour* of the human race (see 1 Tim. 1:1), and " it is his wish that all men should be saved and arrive at knowledge of the truth " (1 Tim. 2:4). This call to salvation, which is addressed to every single person, does not depend on whether a man is worthy of it or

not; it is quite independent of anything a man may achieve and depends completely on God's unmerited gift of grace. It is made as a result of "his own decision, his own graciousness." This call is holy, because it comes from a God who is holy and is aimed at making human beings holy.

2. In accordance with God's eternal plan of salvation, all his saving activity is centered *in Jesus Christ*; he brought it to fulfillment at the time appointed by God. The words "before all ages" underline the eternal character of God's saving will which is expressed once and for all in Jesus Christ. "He chose us out in him [Christ] before the foundation of the world, so that we might be holy and guiltless in his sight. In love, he predestined us to be his children through Jesus Christ, in accordance with his own good pleasure, to exalt the glory of the grace with which he favored us in his beloved Son" (Eph. 1:4–6). God's saving activity in Jesus Christ was revealed at the time appointed by God, that is, "now." As a result of his "epiphany," his "appearing," in the incarnation, in his life on earth, and in his passion and death on the cross, it has become visible to the whole world.

3. One effect of the redemption Jesus Christ brings is that *death has been overcome.* "Death is swallowed up in victory. Death, where is your victory? Death, where is your sting?" (1 Cor. 15:54f.). "We know, indeed, that Christ, after rising from the dead, does not die any more. Death has no more power over him" (Rom. 6:9). Another effect of this redemption is that it brings new life and *immortality.* "We believe that if we have died with Christ, we shall also live with him" (Rom. 6:8). Death's unchallenged reign was destroyed by the redeeming death of Christ on the cross. The darkness which had previously overshadowed the whole human race was dispelled by the light of

life and immortality shed by the gospel. " Sin had imposed its dominion by means of death; in the same way, grace must reign supreme as the result of justification for eternal life, through Jesus Christ our Lord " (Rom. 5:21). Christians have access to this life by faith in the gospel. It is the gospel which makes known the message of God's work of redemption and enables us to share in God's power which it enshrines (see Rom. 1:16). The gifts Jesus gave to Christians on the occasion of his first " epiphany," the incarnation, were victory over death and the offer of new life; and these are the gifts he will bring with him at his second coming, when he returns at the end of time.

11*. . . of which I was appointed a herald, an apostle, and a teacher.* 12*It is for this that I endure this present suffering, but I am not ashamed; I know in whom I have put my trust, and I am convinced that he has the power to keep what was entrusted to me safe until that day.*

Paul has outlined God's saving activity in the history of salvation and thereby described the content of the gospel in a few brief sentences. This is a work of God's power which is almost beyond the grasp of human understanding. As Paul thinks of it, he can refer with pride and joy to the fact that he was entrusted with the preaching of this gospel as its *herald, apostle, and teacher* (see 1 Tim. 2:7). He is the " herald " who announced the good news solemnly to the whole world with the incredible message of happiness it brings. He is an " apostle," an authorized spokesman, who was commissioned by Jesus Christ to bring this message to all mankind. He is a " teacher " whose duty it was to teach the whole world about God's saving activity and his redeeming love. It is true that his imprisonment has narrowed the field in which he can exercise his calling, but it has not done away with it; "God's word cannot be chained" (2:9).

Paul now turns his thoughts to his own position; instead of thinking about the message of the gospel, he thinks about himself. A greater contrast it would be difficult to imagine. The "herald, apostle, and teacher" of this glorious message which comes from God wears fetters and is imprisoned like any ordinary criminal (2:9); he is forced to bear the disgrace of an ordinary offender. Timothy knows what he has to endure as a prisoner; he knows that he endures it all for the sake of the gospel. However, Paul is *not ashamed* of his bonds. Indeed, he wears them with pride. Even in his hours of deepest abandonment in his captivity, he finds all his peace and all his security in God.

The repetition "I know," "I am convinced" proclaims Paul's unshakable confidence which is firmly rooted in his Lord and God. It is not in a human being that he has "put his trust"; it is in the Lord God. His confidence will never be betrayed. He has now come to the end of his days, and his life lies in pieces around him. Yet he is firmly convinced that what was entrusted to him (see 1:14; 1 Tim. 6:20), that is, the gospel which he preached, is safe and sound in God's all-powerful hands "until that day," until the end of the world and Christ's second coming (1:18; 2 Thess. 1:10).

It was only at God's command that Paul had preached the gospel. Now that he has been condemned to inactivity and his life is coming to an end, God will ensure that faith in the gospel will never be destroyed. His messengers will proclaim the gospel farther afield, "to the ends of the earth" (Rom. 10:18). In the hour of his greatest powerlessness and his deepest humiliation, Paul expresses unlimited and completely unshakable *trust in God,* and a firm *conviction* that God's cause will be *victorious.* Only a man who was firmly grounded in God and had given himself completely to him could be filled with such assured confidence.

Hold Fast to the Teaching Handed Down (1:13–14)

13 *As an example of sound doctrine, hold fast to what you have heard from me, in the faith and love which are rooted in Christ Jesus.*
14 *Keep safe the glorious deposit with which you have been entrusted, through the Holy Spirit who lives in us.*

The message which Timothy heard from Paul must be an "example" of "sound doctrine" for his own preaching. Paul here refers to the teaching of Christianity as sound doctrine because it is the perfect expression of spiritual and moral health. It is free from every germ of spiritual disease and inspires a healthy and morally sound life, so that it keeps a man in good health interiorly. Anything which falsifies the teaching of the gospel is diseased. It contains the germs of disease and leads to a dissolute life. Timothy must "hold fast," without reservation, to the doctrine his teacher and master proclaimed. In sincere faith and fervent love, which are rooted in Christ Jesus, he is constantly united with Paul; they will guide him safely.

Paul sums up his appeal with the brief command: *Keep safe the glorious deposit with which you have been entrusted,* the gospel of Jesus Christ. He must ensure that it is proclaimed unceasingly; he must not change it, or add anything to it, or take anything away from it. It is God's word and it is sacrosanct. The Holy Spirit will give him the strength he needs for this difficult task. He lives continually in him, just as he lives in every Christian. He will supplement his natural powers with new, supernatural strength and bring them to perfection.

Paul's Bitter Disappointment; Onesiphorus Is Praised for His Loyalty (1:15–18)

His Bitter Experiences in Asia (1 : 15)

15You know how everyone in Asia abandoned me, among them Phigellus and Hermogenes.

Paul now describes some of the details surrounding his desperate plight. Timothy was aware of his position (" You know ") and these references were quite intelligible to him. However, Paul's words are not precise enough to allow us to make any definite inference. At the same time, it is clear that the Christians from the Roman province of Asia in Asia Minor had abandoned him. This does not necessarily mean that they had abandoned the Christian faith. Very probably it means only that all these Christians had abandoned him, because he was in prison and they were ashamed of him. It is quite conceivable that they may have refused to speak up for him at his trial in Rome, or they may have deserted him at the moment of his arrest. Bitterly disillusioned, Paul sadly mentions two people by name, Phigellus and Hermogenes, of whom we have no further knowledge. They may have been particularly important or influential people, from whom Paul could have expected more. Or it may be that their disloyalty was a particular source of disappointment and discouragement to him. Do these words conceal an appeal to Timothy, his beloved son (1:2), that he at least should not desert him now?

Even in the earliest days of Christianity, therefore, we meet all the *weakness and human frailty* of Christians. In the day of battle, in the hour of need or of danger, they abandon the church and her ministers; they have not the courage to profess their loyalty to the Christian community. This had been Jesus' own experience in the case of many of his followers, after his discourse at Capharnaum (see Jn. 6:66f.). At the time of his arrest at Gethsemani, he had the same experience in the case of his chosen apostles, which was an even greater disappointment (Mt. 26:56; Mk. 14:50). So, too, Paul must suffer the same disillusionment; "a disciple is not above his master" (Mt. 10:24).

Onesiphorus' Loyalty (1:16–18)

16*May God grant mercy to Onesiphorus' family; he repeatedly gave me fresh heart and was not ashamed of my bonds.* 17*When he arrived in Rome, he searched for me eagerly and found me.*
18*The Lord grant that he will find mercy from his Lord on that day! You know better than anyone the services he rendered in Ephesus.*

The *loyalty* of Onesiphorus stands out all the more splendidly against the dark background of the preceding verses. His attitude is now contrasted with that of the Christians who had been unfaithful and their behavior in Asia. He was not afraid and he refused to be ashamed of Paul in his chains. After his arrival in Rome, he searched for Paul "eagerly" and with perseverance;

even the Christians of the church at Rome did not know where Paul was. When he finally located him, he gave him " fresh heart " and strengthened him spiritually and physically.

Even as an apostle and pastor, Paul remained completely and utterly human. So now he is touched to the very depths of his heart at the thought of the true love Onesiphorus had shown him. In his gratitude, he prays that he and his whole family will experience *the Lord's mercy*. The form in which this wish for Onesiphorus (1:16) and his family (1:18) is expressed suggests that this faithful friend of Paul's was already dead at the time the letter was written (see 4:19). May Christ " the Lord grant that he will find mercy from his Lord," that is, God the Father as the Supreme Judge, " on that day," the day of Christ's second coming. With a delightful play on words (He " found " him in Rome, now may he " find " mercy), Paul prays that Onesiphorus will find a merciful Judge in eternity, who will reward him for all his loyalty. With these words, which are like the inscription on a tombstone, Paul raises a wonderful monument of gratitude to his dead friend.

Onesiphorus had also merited well of the church at Ephesus. No one was in a better position to realize that than Timothy who now headed the community as Paul's representative. That was why Paul needed to say nothing more. Through the " services " which he rendered, Onesiphorus left behind him in the church at Ephesus the memory of a strong Christian personality.

Even in the earliest days of the church, therefore, we meet light and shade. In this passage we have an example of the unselfishness of one Christian in the service of the community and his unswerving loyalty to Paul who was chained and held in prison like a criminal. On the other hand, we see the faithlessness and cowardice of others towards him in his hour of need, when he was arrested. As long as it is in its pilgrim state here on this earth, there will always be light and shade in Christ's church, because it is made up of weak human beings. However, faith is capable of bearing even the most bitter disappointments.

Paul Calls on Timothy to Hand On the Tradition Received from the Apostles and Exhorts Him Once More to Be Willing to Suffer (2:1–13)

The Transmission of What Has Been Received From the Apostle to Men Who Could Be Trusted (2:1–2)

[1]*Be strong, my son, in the faith which is founded in Christ Jesus.*

Paul has reached the evening of his life and he sees the churches he had founded threatened with heresy. That is why he is particularly worried about Timothy's steadfastness and loyalty to the faith. As in an earlier passage (1:2) he addresses him affectionately in a fatherly tone as his "son." It is for the same reason that he exhorts him to be strong and not lose heart; he must not yield to timidity, to which he was in fact inclined (see 1:6–8, 13f.). The *grace* which is founded in Christ Jesus must be the source of his strength and his courage. Christ had merited them for him, to save him and make him a present of them (1:6, 14). Through these gifts, he is constantly united with Christ as the source of all his strength.

[2]*What you heard from me in the presence of many witnesses, you must entrust to men who are reliable and capable of teaching others as well.*

Another anxiety of Paul's is that Timothy should entrust the truths of the faith to other Christians on whom he could rely. He himself had received them from Paul and was bound to preserve them from all corruption; now he must transmit the deposit of faith to others who will be able to hand it on to those who listen to them in their turn. The message they bear must be the genuine Christian tradition. Paul remarks that Timothy had heard these truths *in the presence of many witnesses,* probably in the course of a solemn function during which he formally entrusted the teachings of the faith to him. Did this take place, perhaps, at a meeting of the whole community, during which Timothy was installed as head of the church at Ephesus and received the profession of faith? Or was it on the occasion of the imposition of hands (see 1:6; 1 Tim. 6:12), when he received the grace of office and made a solemn profession of faith, while the presbyters who assisted confirmed the Christian teaching by their faithful testimony? St. Paul's remark is an important proof of how the teachings of the faith were preserved and handed down. A firm bond of tradition unites our faith with the message that Paul himself preached and ultimately with the teaching of Christ.

An Appeal for Readiness to Suffer as Christ's Soldier (2:3–7)

[3]*As a loyal soldier of Jesus Christ, you must share his sufferings.*
[4]*No one who serves as a soldier allows himself to become entangled with the affairs of ordinary life, so that he will please his commanding officer.* [5]*An athlete entered for a contest will win the crown of victory, only if he observes the rules of the contest.*
[6]*The farmer who has worked hard must be given the first share*

of the harvest. [7]*Grasp what I am saying. The Lord will grant you understanding in all circumstances.*

Paul had already reminded Timothy in his first letter that he had been enlisted as a soldier in the service of Jesus Christ (1 Tim. 1:18; 4:10). As a " loyal soldier of Jesus Christ " it is not enough that he should be prepared to fight and to struggle, together with Paul his teacher and model; he must also be prepared to suffer. He must share Christ's sufferings and bear courageously all the shame and hardship which preaching the gospel brings him. It seems that in this passage Paul wants to remind his disciple of Jesus' words: " Remember what I said to you. A servant is not greater than his lord. If they have persecuted me, they will also persecute you " (Jn. 15:20).

The sincere imitation of Christ implies *willingness to endure suffering* on the part of all Christians. Only complete and absolute determination to follow Christ closely, accompanied by the courageous acceptance of all hardships and difficulties, can lead a Christian to his goal. Paul brings this lesson home to his disciple in three similes.

A *soldier* on active service must devote himself to his duty wholeheartedly, with every reserve of strength he has. Consequently, he must be free from all the activities necessary for earning a living, which would distract him from his real task. This is the only way he can hope to satisfy the commanding officer who enlisted him. In the same way, Timothy must dedicate all his powers unreservedly to the service of the gospel. He must not engage in other duties which would take him away or distract him from this, his most important duty. It is only by so doing that he will earn the approval of Jesus Christ, his Lord who is in heaven.

The second simile refers to an *athlete*. An athlete entered for a contest in the arena will win the laurel of victory from the adjudicator only if he observes the rules of the contest carefully and does not transgress them. So, too, in preaching the gospel of Jesus Christ, Timothy cannot follow a path of his own choosing. He must not make the slightest change in the deposit of faith entrusted to him. He may not compromise, to make his task easier; he must remain true to the wishes and directives which come from Jesus Christ.

The third comparison Paul hints at is with a *farmer*. A farmer must sweat and toil, if he wants to reap a harvest from his land. Nothing falls into his lap without hard work. Timothy is a laborer employed in God's service. He must not shrink from the toil and effort this involves; he must dedicate himself to his task as an apostle wholeheartedly and with all his strength. Then and only then can he lay claim to the material fruits of his labors here on earth, that is, the upkeep the church affords him (see 1 Cor. 9:7). Above all, however, it is only such unremitting toil which will enable him to share in the spiritual and heavenly fruits of his labor on God's great harvest day, when Christ comes again. An apostle who dedicates himself wholly to the service of the gospel earns Jesus' special love; he will reward him for everything.

Paul is content to outline his similes very briefly. He does not go into details and he purposely avoids applying them to Timothy. Is he being tactful? Is he unwilling to make his wishes clearer? He leaves it to Timothy himself to meditate and reflect on what he has said and draw his own conclusions. God's grace will come to his aid and enlighten him, so that he will see what is demanded of him in the circumstances.

Jesus' Resurrection (2:8–13)

8 *Think of Jesus Christ who comes from the seed of David, who was raised from the dead, according to the gospel I preach.*
9 *Therein lies the reason why I suffer and am in chains, like a criminal. However, God's word is not fettered.*

The memory of Jesus Christ should have a greater influence on Timothy than any image or any comparison drawn from human life. That is why Paul turns his thoughts to "Jesus Christ who comes from the seed of David, who was raised from the dead." These words have a stereotyped ring about them and they probably come from an early Christian profession of faith or perhaps a baptismal hymn. Jesus Christ who came from the tribe of David according to his human birth, as had already been foretold in the Old Testament, was the centerpiece of the gospel St. Paul preached. The emphasis, however, is on the phrase "who was raised from the dead." He was the Messiah whom God rescued from the kingdom of death, after he had suffered the agony of his passion and had been put to death on the cross like a criminal. In this way, he was revealed as the source of eternal life and the rightful heir to the dignity of the messianic kingdom. As such, he must be the center of all of Timothy's thoughts and actions. Christ gained access to eternal glory only by means of his passion and cross. This is also the way to salvation indicated for Timothy. The thought of Jesus in his passion and death, as also the thought of him in his resurrection and glory, provides every Christian with something to which he can cling fast, an unshakable set of principles, in all the circumstances of his life.

This was the gospel that Paul preached and this was the

reason why he now had to suffer, as he languished in prison and felt the shame of being treated like a criminal. In his hours of loneliness and desolation, he too fixed his eyes on the crucified Messiah. By God's power, he had passed over from the kingdom of death to the glory of the resurrection. This was the source of Paul's perseverance and his hope.

Although he was in chains and detained in prison against his will, a joyful cry of victory wrests itself from Paul's heart. This is the good news, the proclamation that *God's word is not fettered*. It was being broadcast ever further afield in the world and no human power could stop it (see 4:17). He had already written, during his first imprisonment, "Most of the Christians have taken courage in the Lord from my chains and are to preach God's word all the more fearlessly" (Phil. 1:14). Paul was probably thinking of the unflinching courage of his fellow missionaries who preached the gospel in Galatia and Dalmatia (4:10). It is possible that he also had in mind the sufferings he himself endured in prison for the gospel; this too was a form of service in favor of God's word.

10 *Therefore, I endure everything for the sake of the elect, that they too may attain salvation in Jesus Christ and eternal glory as well.*

Paul can no longer carry on his apostolic work actively in the churches he had founded; he is restricted by limitations he cannot escape. Yet he still has one means at his disposal whereby he can make his influence felt. This is *his suffering*. Suffering, too, forms part of his vocation as an apostle. By means of his suffering, he can act vicariously on behalf of all those whom God has called to salvation, whom he has chosen and summoned to the faith, in accordance with his own unfathomable design. Such intercession also benefits those who have already received the gift of faith in the waters of baptism. Finally, it will help those who have yet to be called by God, so that they may all attain salvation and its final crowning in the glory of eternal life. Of course, Jesus Christ will always remain the ultimate course of their salvation, their redemption, and their "eternal glory." Paul is firmly convinced that his suffering is of value to the whole church, the whole body of Christ; that the suffering of one member benefits all the members of Christ's body. All Christians form a "communion of saints." In this way, the sufferings he endures unseen in prison transcend the walls of his cell and promote the spread of the gospel and the salvation of all men.

11 *This saying deserves to be believed:*
If we have died with him,
we shall also live with him.
12 *If we persevere,*
we shall also share his reign;
if we deny him,
he will also deny us.
13 *If we are unfaithful,*
he remains faithful;
he cannot deny himself.

A hymn overflowing with fervent hope forms the conclusion of Paul's exhortation. It is introduced with a conventional formula and is probably taken from the liturgy of baptism. The first two strophes are devoted to our union with Christ and the reward this union brings. The second two, by way of contrast, speak of separation from Christ and unfaithfulness towards him, and of the consequences of such disloyalty.

Anyone who loses his life for Christ and dies with him will live for ever with him in eternal glory. When he speaks of sharing Christ's death, is Paul thinking of a *dying with* him in a moral sense, the death to sin which is accomplished in the waters of baptism? Or should his words be taken literally as referring to that sharing in Christ's death which is found in martyrdom? It may be that he wants to underline what is essential in martyrdom; it is a form of suffering and death endured "with him," with Christ. Is this the view he takes of his own imprisonment and the death which faces him? Does he look upon his death as something which will enable him to share in the glorified life of Jesus Christ, the risen Lord? Patience and perseverance in suffering are his assurance of one day sharing in Christ's kingly power. Union with Christ in death, therefore, leads to union with him in eternal life; sharing in his passion leads to an eternal sharing in his royal dominion.

But what happens if a Christian fails to live up to his ideals? If he abandons Christ and renounces him? If we deny Christ during our life, in our hour of difficulty or trial, he will *deny us* at the last judgment. "If anyone denies me before men, I will also deny him before my Father in heaven" (Mt. 10:33), Jesus tells us. If a Christian lacks the courage of his convictions, if he refuses to acknowledge his Lord in the trials and sufferings of life, Christ too will refuse to acknowledge him at the last judgment, when God's mercy is the only thing on which he could pin his hope. Paul's words are intended to lend weight to his appeal and make Timothy conscious of the gravity of the question. However, his train of thought now takes a peculiar turn.

If a Christian goes a step further and is "unfaithful"—here

the contrast is underlined far more emphatically—*Christ remains faithful nonetheless.* Indeed, he could not do otherwise; he cannot be untrue to himself or deny his own word and his own being. Christ counters the Christian's infidelity with his divine fidelity. Does this mean that Christ behaves towards the faithless Christian as a just judge who remains true to his threat of eternal damnation and is determined to carry it out? Or is the sense that the Christian's denial and infidelity are overcome by Christ's love and fidelity? This interpretation is more likely. In his ineffable mercy and his unfathomable love, Christ does not reject the Christian who has fallen. Instead, like a good shepherd, he lovingly seeks out the sheep that has strayed and, when he has found it, brings it back rejoicing (see Lk. 15:4–6). A Christian's weakness, his denial or infidelity will always find something it can cling fast to in the fidelity and forgiving love of his Lord, Jesus Christ, whose mercy is inexhaustible.

THE PROPER ATTITUDE TOWARDS HERETICS (2:14—4:8)

In the second part of his letter Paul gives Timothy instructions on how to deal with heretics. He warns him, first of all, against entering into wordy disputes with them or giving ear to their empty talk. Indeed, this would only lead to further godlessness and finally to apostasy from the faith. He points out, by way of contrast, that the foundation God has laid, Christ's church, can never be shaken (2:14–21).

He then appeals to Timothy to bring back the Christians who had strayed, not by disputing with them, but by instructing them in a spirit of charity and by the example of a Christian life (2:22–26). The activities of the heretics must not throw Timothy or the other Christians into confusion. Such moral degeneration has been foretold for the last stage of time and it has already begun in them (3:1–9). Timothy's duty consists in remaining faithful to Paul's teaching and the example of his life; he must hold fast with inalterable firmness to the truths revealed in sacred scripture (3:10–17). This involves indefatigable zeal in preaching God's word and complete dedication to the service of the truth, particularly now that Paul's death is imminent (4:1–8).

A Warning Against Useless Disputes and Empty Talk (2:14–21)

A Warning Against Disputes (2:14–15)

14*Remind them of this, enjoining upon them before God not*

to dispute with empty words. Such disputes benefit no one and, indeed, they can lead to the downfall of those who are listening.

Paul introduces his instructions with an appeal to Timothy never to let his Christians forget the truths of salvation which he has described in the preceding verses (2:8–13). Jesus Christ who was raised from the dead after the humiliation of his passion and death on the cross and entered into glory, must be at the heart of the message he preaches. Unswerving loyalty to Christ, in life and in death, will bring Christians to their full achievement and enable them to share in Christ's royal dominion. Timothy must be particularly emphatic in warning them seriously against *disputes* with the heretics. Such controversies do no good; the heretics are not converted and those who hear them are often led astray (see 1 Tim. 6:20f.).

Such disputes do nothing to further love of God or one's neighbor; they advance no one on the way to salvation. Indeed, they often do nothing more than create new problems and frequently lead to " the downfall of those who are listening."

15*Make it your aim to prove yourself in God's eyes, as a worker who has nothing to be ashamed of, who proclaims the message of truth faithfully.*

The important thing is not superiority in controversy with the heretics; it is fidelity in *preaching the gospel.* Timothy's whole duty consists in " proclaiming the message of the truth faithfully." The gospel is the " message of truth " because it contains the revelation God has made to us in Christ. If Timothy fulfills this task, he will " prove " himself a capable worker and God will be his judge.

A Warning Against Empty Talk (2:16–18)

[16]*Avoid profane and empty speeches; the heretics will fall ever deeper into a state of godlessness,* [17a]*and their words will eat into everything about them like a cancer.*

Paul once more repeats his exhortation to *avoid profane, empty speeches.* He scorns the heretics' speculations, which were inspired by spiritual pride, as so much empty talk. The message they proclaimed was not " the message of truth "; they wanted to substitute their human ideas for the gospel revealed by God. That is why their words are " profane " and " empty." Unfortunately things will become even worse. The heretics will fall deeper into a state of godlessness; they will wander further and further away from the revealed truth and will finally be separated from God more completely than ever. Heresy will spread like a malignant cancer in the church; it will stifle healthy religious and moral forces in the entire community and finally kill them; and so it will lead to the downfall of the community.

[17b]*Among them belong Hymenaeus and Philetas.* [18]*They have strayed from the truth by saying that the resurrection has already taken place and they are destroying the faith of many others.*

Paul mentions two of the heretics by name: Hymenaeus, whom he had already excluded from the Christian community (1 Tim. 1:20) and who must have been one of their leaders; and Philetas, about whom we know nothing further. He gives a brief outline of the heresy they preached. They maintained that the resurrection had already taken place. It is probable that they interpreted the resurrection *in a purely spiritual sense.* Consequently, they denied that our bodies would rise to a new immortal life of glory (see 1 Cor. 15:20–24) which will be inaugurated only in the future, when our salvation is fully accomplished. Anyone who places the resurrection in the past, at the moment of baptism, is found to exclude the resurrection and glorification of the body. This heresy was based ultimately on a false conception of the human body and an attitude of hostility towards it. It was a perversion of Paul's teaching on the resurrection and he rightly regarded it as undermining Christian revelation in its entirety. This heresy was obviously in keeping with the Greek way of thinking (see 1 Cor. 15; Acts 17:32), and we may ask ourselves whether it had already been widely accepted in the Christian church, that Paul should compare it to a cancer which ate into everything around it?

Paul sees clearly the great danger this heresy represented for the faith and the existence of the community. That is why he warns Timothy so urgently. Even at this early stage in the history of the church, the tares which the enemy had sown among the wheat (Mt. 13:25) were already to be seen. Heretical doctrines had made their appearance; they were spreading dangerously and threatened the church. Paul was under no illusion; his anxiety for the Christians entrusted to him never left him and he was especially anxious now that his death was imminent, and so he delivers this warning.

God's Firm Foundation (2:19–21)

[19]*However, God's firm foundation remains unshaken and it*

bears this inscription: The Lord knows his own (Num. 16:5), *and: Everyone who calls on the name of the Lord must keep clear of all wrong-doing* (Is. 26:13).

Even if heresy is spreading destructively like a cancer and even if individual members of the community have lost the faith, the truth of the Christian faith is not thereby threatened in its existence; it rests *on God's firm foundation*, the church (see 1 Tim. 3:15). It remains unaffected, despite the activities of the heretics. In antiquity, it was customary to have dedicatory inscriptions on temples and houses. In the same way, Paul sees two inscriptions carved on God's foundation, the church, of which they give us a clear and accurate description.

The first inscription (taken from Num. 16:5) underlines the security that this foundation—that is, the church—enjoys in God's love. *God knows his own*, all those who live and dwell in this foundation. He loves them, protects them, and defends them. Everybody who lives in this foundation belongs to God and enjoys his unfailing protection and love.

The second inscription is made up of phrases taken from the Old Testament and it points out the duty imposed on all who live in this house; they must be free from *sin and wrong-doing*. Every Christian, everyone who reverently invokes God's name in prayer and so acknowledges his faith in him, must keep far from all sin. This makes it clear that God's firm foundation is his holy church, which he guards with such love. Timothy must remember this comforting truth. Christians must never forget the security they enjoy in God's loving protection; they must never be anxious or downcast, even if great numbers abandon the faith. Even if the church encounters serious interior or exterior difficulties, "God's firm foundation remains unshaken."

[20]*In a great mansion, all the utensils are not gold or silver; some are made of wood or earthenware. Some are used for honorable purposes, others for less honorable purposes.* [21]*If, then, a person keeps himself clean from these, he will become an instrument capable of being put to honorable use; he will be sanctified and useful to the Lord, ready for every good work.*

The appearance of heretics and the fact that opposition from the Evil One was to be met in God's own house is not surprising; it must not make Timothy or the other Christians deviate from the true faith. Paul explains this by comparing the church, God's house, to a great *household* which contains utensils of the most varied kinds (see Rom. 9:21). These are distinguished, for one thing, by the material of which they are made (they are of " gold or silver, wood or earthenware "). But they are also distinguished by reason of the purpose they were made to serve. There are utensils which are destined for honorable use, and others which will be employed less honorably. In the same way, the Christians who are united in a single community, God's house, perform different services. This is in keeping with God's design, to which Christians must submit with all humility (see Rom. 9:14–30); they have no right to quibble at it or find fault with it.

If a person is given to " empty disputes " (2:14) or " profane and empty speeches," he is an instrument destined for " dishonorable and worthless uses." If, on the other hand, he keeps himself untainted by the danger of heresy and tears himself away from the path which leads to godlessness (2:16), he becomes an instrument which can be put to honorable use in God's hands. Then he is useful to the Lord; he is a suitable instrument in his hand, one which can be put to " any good work " God's grace wishes to perform in him. To be a useful instrument in God's hands will always be a Christian's most important task. He must be constantly at God's disposal, as our Lord said of himself: "My food is to do the will of him who sent me" (Jn. 4:34).

Paul Appeals to Timothy to Lead an Exemplary Christian Life and Instruct Those Who Have Strayed in a Spirit of Charity (2:22–26)

An Appeal for a Genuinely Christian Life (2:22–23)

22*Beware of all youthful passions. Make holiness, faith, and love your aim, and peace with all those who call upon the Lord with a clean heart.* 23*You must shun this silly and ill-informed gossiping; you know it only leads to quarreling.*

Paul calls upon Timothy to struggle valiantly against the heretics; heresy must be excluded, once and for all, from the Christian community. In this, his personal behavior as a Christian will play a decisive role. The more clearly his whole personality appears penetrated with the spirit of Jesus Christ, and the more enthusiastically his whole being is engaged in preaching the gospel, the more successful will be his campaign against the heretics. This will also make it easier for him to show those Christians who have been led astray the right way to repentance.

That is why Paul appeals to him *to beware of all youthful passions*. We know from 1 Timothy (4:12) that Timothy was still a young man when he was appointed head of the church at Ephesus. This involved the danger that he might allow himself to be influenced by his youthful impetuosity, his " youthful passions," in his dealings with the heretics. Paul, therefore, warns him to rid himself of all the faults young people so easily fall into in the heat of controversy. These are sensitiveness, passionate or excessive zeal, irritability, imprudence, and excessive ardor in general.

He must set an example of all the virtues which govern his relations with God and with men. He must be firmly established in unshakable faith; *holiness and love* must be all his aim, and especially peace with all Christians (Christians are those who " call upon the Lord with a clean heart "). A genuinely Christian life such as this helps to bind the community together.

For the third time, Paul once more exhorts Timothy to " shun silly and ill-informed gossiping." We must conclude from the repetition of the warning that there was a great danger Timothy would engage in such discussions. He must simply refuse to occupy himself with them. He must *shun* all such controversies, once and for all. They only lead to quarreling. Such disputes are incompatible with a Christian life, the characteristic mark of which must be sincere charity.

Instruct Those Who Have Strayed in a Spirit of Charity (2:24–26)

24 A servant of the Lord must not engage in disputes; he must be friendly towards all men and capable of instructing them. He must be patient 25 and correct those who are obstinate with all gentleness, in the hope that God will grant them a change of heart and bring them to knowledge of the truth. 26 Then they will come back to their right minds, freed from the snares of the devil whose prisoners they were, so that they will be at the disposal of God's will.

As a Christian and especially as the head of the community, Timothy is a " servant of the Lord "; he is completely dedicated to God and has consecrated his whole life to him. Moreover, like the great men of Israel (Abraham, Moses, David, Isaiah), he has been chosen by God for a special mission. As God's servant, he must not engage in " disputes." The sharp-tongued or spirited refutation of their arguments is not the way to bring back to repentance Christians who have gone astray. Far more effective is that charity which is kind and gentle towards everyone and bears injuries with patience. Those who have strayed must be given a sympathetic hearing and instructed gently (see 1 Cor. 13:4–7). Charity which is both *merciful and understanding* prepares the way for God's grace to penetrate the hearts of those in error and bring them to conversion. Then they will come to " knowledge of the truth." That is why a gentle, kindly, and loving attitude on Timothy's part is the best possible preparation for God's grace.

Those who have strayed are still completely beguiled by the ignorance of their own hearts. They have been trapped in Satan's snares; they have no will of their own and are completely at his disposal, like wild animals caught in a net. Paul, therefore, sees Satan's influence at work behind the heretics; he sows tares among the wheat (see Mt. 13:25f.). The heretics are the instruments of the Evil One. That is why he appeals to Timothy to struggle manfully and avoid being caught up in controversies and disputes; his resistance must be practical and effective; in his personal behavior, he must have charity and understanding and compassionate love for his fellow Christians who are in error. So he will prepare the way for God's activity; only God can inspire men's hearts and bring them back to their "right mind." Then they will wake up and throw off Satan's snares. The greatest means a Christian has for preparing the way for God's grace to penetrate the hearts of those who have strayed is self-sacrificing love for his fellow men.

The Activities of the Heretics as the Beginning of the Final Corruption to Come (3:1–9)

Paul Foretells the Moral Degeneracy to Come at the End of Time (3:1–5)

[1]*You must know that in the last stage of time there will be periods of great difficulty.* [2]*People will be selfish, avaricious, boastful, proud, and given to slander; they will be disobedient to their parents, ungrateful, godless,* [3]*loveless, implacable, backbiters, unbridled, undisciplined, enemies of all that is good;* [4]*they will be treacherous, reckless, arrogant, more intent on their own satisfaction than on pleasing God.* [5a]*They will assume an appearance of religion, while refusing to acknowledge its power.*

Paul turns his thoughts from the present to the future; to the *last stage of time,* the end of the world, when moral decay of every kind will spread frighteningly in all directions (see 1 Tim. 4:1–5). This is the result of abandoning the truth. In the heresy which was spreading like a cancer at Ephesus (2:17), he sees in germ the beginning of this general moral decay which will make its appearance at the end of time. In this composite picture, therefore, Paul's experiences in the present are coupled with a prophetic view of the future. This is in keeping with the expectation of a great apostasy to come, which is already making its influence felt in a hidden way. Paul's intention obviously is to show where the heretics' opposition to God's revealed truth will ultimately lead. The " last stage of time " is the period which precedes Christ's second coming; it is then that the trials and afflictions promised for the end of time will make their appearance. Then " lawlessness will prevail and the charity of many people will grow cold." In Paul's view, the trials and tribulations of the last stage of time, the " periods of great difficulty " that he speaks of, will be occasioned not by cosmic disasters, but by an increase of wickedness in every form. This will be such as to destroy all morality and religion, and make it impossible for human beings to live in peace.

He paints a frightening picture of the corruption of mankind. Selfishness and greed (see 1 Tim. 6:10) are the source of the general decay of the human race. *Unrestrained self-seeking* will assert itself recklessly. Arrogance in one's approach to God and the complete lack of any real love for one's fellow men, even the closest members of one's family, are the natural results. This will be accompanied by widespread hypocrisy and deceit. All the outward signs of religion will remain, but the reality will be lacking.

5b*You must avoid such people!*

In Paul's mind, the beginnings of this universal moral corruption are already to be seen in the heretics and their activities in the community. With this thought, he leaves his description of the future to return to the present. Briefly and to the point, he warns Timothy, "You must avoid such people!" What is needed is a complete *break* with the heretics. The time has come to draw a clear dividing-line between the community and the heretics with their fanaticism. It is striking how emphatically Paul insists on a complete break being made between Christians and the heretics. There can be no question of entering into discussion or controversy with them (see 2:14, 16, 23); there must be no attempt at compromise. What is needed is complete separation between light and darkness, between Christ and Belial (see 2 Cor. 6:15); the heretics are Satan's tools (see 2:26).

The Activities of the Heretics as the Beginning of This Corruption (3:6–9)

6From among them come those who make their way furtively from house to house and entrap women of low repute who are burdened with sins and allow themselves to be ruled by lusts of all kinds.
7They are for ever learning but can never reach knowledge of the truth.

Paul now attacks the conduct of some of the heretics with biting words. He obviously has in mind certain incidents which had taken place in the church at Ephesus. There the heretics concentrated their attention on the women members of the church, to win them to their cause. This they did secretly ("furtively"), not openly, because they feared for their good name. Paul indicates the women he is thinking of more accurately by saying that they were "burdened with sins." Their past life was not beyond reproach and they "allow themselves to be ruled by lusts of all kinds." They had not completely abandoned their sinful inclinations. However, they were inquisitive about new forms of knowledge, and they put forward their great interest in religion as an excuse; they were "for ever learning." Yet they never arrived at knowledge of the real truth. They were not really serious about their efforts to achieve salvation. They had no wish to lead a genuinely Christian life and they were not prepared to be humble and take Christ's message seriously. Despite all their interest in religion, they never attained true faith in Christ, that is, *knowledge of the truth*.

[8]*Jannes and Jambres opposed Moses; in the same way, these people set themselves up in opposition to the truth, with their depraved spirits and their lack of instruction in the faith.* [9]*However, their period of success is at an end; their folly will be clear to everyone, just as the folly of those others was also clearly demonstrated.*

The heretics who went to such lengths to win disciples had once been members of the Christian community. However, their minds had become dull and they had abandoned the truth, as a result of their lack of a genuine and authentic faith. Now they *opposed* God's gospel when it was preached in the community. In this they behaved like Jannes and Jambres, the two magicians we know of from Jewish tradition, who opposed Moses when he approached Pharaoh before delivering the chosen people out of the slavery of Egypt.

On that occasion, however, the two magicians' tricks were easily seen through. In the same way, the heretics' plans in the community will also be brought to nothing. Paul asserts his firm conviction: Their period of success is at an end. Their subversive activity will collapse; it already bears within it the germ of its own destruction, because "their folly will be clear to everyone."

The tares which the Enemy sows in God's field will always be found alongside the good seed. Heretics will always be a threat to the true faith, and even to the existence of the church, in many instances. However, God himself ensures the preservation of the gospel from all adulteration, in keeping with Jesus' promise: "See, I am with you all days until the end of the world" (Mt. 28:20). God's Spirit, on the other hand, ensures the proper development and interpretation of Jesus' message; "he will teach them everything and remind them of everything" (Jn. 14:26), Jesus said. He will ward off all error, because God's fidelity lasts for ever (see Ps. 116:2).

An Appeal for Loyalty and Steadfastness (3:10–17)

Paul Appeals to Timothy to Remain Faithful to the Example of His Life and Teaching (3:10–13)

10 You took as your model the teaching I gave and my way of life, together with my ideals, my faith, my forbearance, my love, my patience. 11 You saw how I was persecuted and all my sufferings, such as I endured in Antioch, Iconium, and Lystra. What persecutions I suffered! And God saved me from them all.

To the heretics and their activities Paul now contrasts the way in which Timothy *imitated* him. He, at least, was on the right path. From the very moment that he had been converted by Paul's preaching, Timothy had taken him as his model in his teaching, in his personal life (faith, forbearance, love, patience), and in all his ideals. He was determined to be a faithful disciple of his master, just as a child likes to imitate his father. He even felt obliged to imitate Paul's readiness to sacrifice himself and his willingness to endure suffering. He was perfectly familiar with the sufferings that Paul encountered on his first missionary journey, to which he refers here. When Paul arrived at Timothy's home town of Lystra on that occasion (Acts 14:6), he had already been driven out of Antioch in Pisidia (Acts 13:50). At Iconium he had barely escaped death by stoning (Acts 14:5f.). In Lystra he was actually stoned and dragged out of the city, where he was left for dead (Acts 14:19). Timothy refused to be frightened by the sufferings and persecutions that Paul had to endure; they did not prevent him from becoming his disciple or from taking him as his model. Even though he was now in prison, Paul looks back at his first missionary journey in a spirit of thankfulness, despite the sufferings it involved at different stages. Insults and persecutions had been his lot in the service of the gospel, yet God's wonderful power never failed to rescue him from all dangers. God is greater and more powerful than the malice of men.

12*In the same way, all those who are determined to live a holy life in Christ Jesus will suffer persecution.*

What Paul experienced holds good for all Jesus' disciples in this world. He states emphatically that all Jesus' followers—the emphasis is on *all*—must suffer, even if their suffering is often restricted to persecutions inflicted upon them from without. We see how much Paul himself had suffered at the hands of his fellow Christians, not to mention what he suffered from others. Paul is very emphatic; must we conclude from this that Timothy and the rest of the community would soon have to undergo persecution? Our Lord himself told us clearly, "You will all be hated for my name's sake" (Mt. 10:22). Jesus' followers do not belong to this world. Consequently, "the world hates them." "Remember what I told you: A servant is not greater than his master. If they have persecuted me, they will also persecute you" (Jn. 15:19f.).

Paul here lays down one of the principles of the Christian life for all those *who are determined to live a holy life in Christ Jesus*. However, the assurance that they will have to suffer must not discourage Christians or make them downcast. "Happy are those who suffer persecution for the sake of holiness; the kingdom of heaven belongs to them. Happy are you when they insult you and persecute you, speaking all kinds of evil against you untruly, for my sake. You must be glad and rejoice; your reward in heaven is great" (Mt. 5:10–12). Therefore, Timothy must not be surprised or dismayed, no matter what persecutions he may have to suffer. The realization that God is on hand to help, accompanied by trust in his support, will give him courage and strength.

[13]*Evil men and impostors will continue to go from bad to worse; they lead others astray and are led astray themselves.*

The thought of the heretics should be a further motive of fidelity and perseverance on the right road for Timothy. They had abandoned the way of faith in Christ. Paul calls them "evil men," because they resisted the truth revealed by God. He calls them "impostors," because they led people into error with their deceitful practices. They have taken the wrong path and it leads them further and further towards complete estrangement from God. They lead others into error and are themselves seduced by falsehood; they will continue to go from bad to worse. They are a *frightening example* for all Christians. However, they show us where abandoning the truth leads to.

An Exhortation to Hold Fast to Sacred Scripture (3:14–17)

[14]*It is for you, however, to hold fast by what you have learned, the teaching of which you are convinced. You know from whom you learned it;* [15]*from childhood you have been acquainted with the sacred scriptures, the source of your wisdom, that wisdom which leads to salvation through the faith which is founded in Christ Jesus.*

In contrast to the heretics, Timothy must hold fast to the tradition of faith handed on by the apostles. This will keep him safe from all error. With the firm conviction born of faith, he had already made his own the teaching he had received in bygone days from Christian missionaries. Two factors should now help to keep him on the path he had taken. One was the memory of his *teachers*. He must not forget who it was that taught him. He had been instructed in the faith from his earliest days by his pious mother Eunice and his grandmother Lois (1:5). These were followed by Paul himself and also other missionaries who gave him further instruction. All his teachers shared a deep faith and it was they who had introduced him to Christianity and the Old Testament which forms its basis.

Another factor from which Timothy must draw strength for his life as a Christian and the conduct of his office is the memory of the *scriptures* with which he was familiar from childhood. From his earliest youth he received instruction in the writings of the Old Testament, in the synagogue and from his mother and grandmother (1:5). These will show him the way to salvation, when they are read in the light of the faith which is revealed and given to us in Jesus Christ and to which we hold fast by communion with him. The scriptures are accomplished in Jesus Christ and, if Timothy allows himself to be guided by the new light faith brings, they will give him a deep insight into God's way of salvation and bring him to eternal life.

[16]*Scripture in its entirety is inspired by God and it can teach,*
reprove, correct, and train us in holiness. [17]*So a man of God*
will be equal to all the demands made of him and prepared for
every kind of good action.

Why are the writings of the Old Testament so vitally important? Because scripture in its entirety is inspired by God, and this includes all the books of the Old Testament. The human authors of these books did not write on their own authority; they wrote as instruments of the Holy Spirit. This means that God himself is the author of the Old Testament. God himself exercises an effective influence on the composition and the contents of the books of sacred scripture. Therefore, it is really God himself who speaks to us in the Bible, so that it is God's word.

Coming from God as it does, scripture contains God's own wisdom to teach and instruct us. For Christians, sacred scripture is God's own means of teaching us his will and converting sinners and those who have strayed. It uplifts those who are in need of conversion and helps them to be better, while it teaches all Christians how to live as God expects them to live, in keeping with his will.

In this way, sacred scripture enables the " man of God " (see

1 Tim. 6:11), that is, anyone who bears office in the community, and also all other Christians, to rise to the demands made of them. They are well prepared for every kind of good action, for every form of active charity. Paul here makes a clear and unequivocal statement concerning the writings of the Old Testament. These books of the Old Testament were composed under the influence of God's Spirit; they are God's inspired word. It is true that it is only when we read these writings in the light of Christ that we see their real meaning. It is only then that they can serve to make Christians more holy. This shows us the love with which a Christian should read sacred scripture and listen to God's word. He must study it carefully and reflect on it, taking it as the norm of his life. Sacred scripture is the source of all Christian training and formation in the faith.

Unwearied Service of the Truth (4:1–8)

Paul Makes an Urgent Appeal to Timothy to Preach God's Word (4:1–4)

[1]I adjure you before God and Jesus Christ, who will judge the living and the dead, by his coming and his kingdom; [2]preach the word, insist on it, whether people like it or not; reprove, correct, and exhort in all patience and instruction.

The nearer we come to the end of the letter, the more urgent Paul's appeals become. He is content to set them down one after another in brief phrases (4:2, 5). This shows us how anxious he was. Timothy must have *courage;* he must be inspired by a sense of duty and prove himself equal to the tasks facing him in the church. In solemn tones, Paul reminds him of the great responsibility which is his (see 1 Tim. 5:21). He arraigns him before God and Jesus Christ, the risen Lord; he is the Supreme Judge who will pass sentence on the actions of all men at the end of time. The Lord will come for the Last Judgment, which will inaugurate his eternal kingdom. Paul reminds Timothy of the judgment of Jesus Christ, the incorruptible Judge. He will judge "the living and the dead," that is, those who are still alive at his second coming and those who have already died, but have been raised to new life. He will also pass the final sentence on Timothy and all his activities in the community.

In the sight of the two supreme judges of the human race, Paul calls upon Timothy to be zealous and preach "the word," God's revelation, with the courage worthy of a man. He must never allow human respect to influence his proclamation of the gospel. It makes no difference whether people like it or not; whether the time, the circumstances, or the manner in which the gospel is preached are suitable or not. It makes no difference even whether people are prepared to open their hearts to this message and accept it humbly, or are determined to reject it. Paul says of himself: "I am under compulsion, and it will be too bad for me, if I do not preach the gospel" (1 Cor. 9:16). Timothy must do his best to correct those who are at fault and have gone astray and bring them to a better frame of mind; he must rebuke them, reproaching them with all seriousness and encouraging them, as the case may be. In all this, his conduct must be inspired by patience and forbearance; he must achieve his purpose by instructing people in a spirit of gentleness, not by a policy of impatience or harshness. He has need of the charity of which Paul says that it is "patient, not jealous, or soured; it does not bear a grudge, but tries to cover up everything, believing, hoping, and enduring all things" (1 Cor. 13:4–7).

[3]*A time will come when they will find it impossible to accept sound doctrine. They will look for teachers after their own tastes, who will give them something to make them prick their ears.* [4]*They will close their ears to the truth and turn to fables instead.*

Such sincere fidelity in preaching God's word is more necessary now than ever; an age is dawning which will see the advent of periods of great difficulty (see 3:1). Indeed, the appearance of the heretics means this age has already begun. People have already turned their backs on "sound doctrine" and shaken it off like an unbearable yoke. They find the earnest proclamation of sin and judgment, of redemption and sanctification intolerable; it does not suit them and it is not to their taste. They are moved by human self-seeking and their own passions. Consequently, they are intent on their own spiritual satisfaction and have ears only for what is clever, interesting, or sensational. They go from teacher to teacher, changing from one to another. There is no scarcity of teachers who propagate doctrines calculated to make them prick their ears.

What are the consequences of such behavior? They will close their ears to the truth. They will exchange God's truth for baseless fables and empty rumors invented by human beings. Paul draws a sharp contrast between God's revealed truth and the purely human elaborations of the heretics. This gives us some idea of the danger these constituted for the community and of Timothy's obligation to preach God's word in the faithful discharge of his duty, without tiring. That is why Paul is so anxious.

Wholehearted Devotion to the Service of the Truth (4:5–8)

[5]*It is for you, on the other hand, to adopt a sober attitude in every way and put up with hardship. You must do the work of an evangelist, fulfilling your duty perfectly and completely.*

In contrast to the heretics with their fantasies, Timothy must be balanced; he must allow himself to be guided by charity and discretion in preaching the gospel. There is no doubt that preaching God's word involves having to bear insults and hardship. Timothy knows this from Paul's life and the persecutions he endured (see 3:11). As the Apostle's "true son" (1 Tim. 1:2; see 2 Tim. 1:2), he must *endure* such hostility *courageously*. As an "evangelist," that is, one entrusted with the proclamation of the gospel, his sphere of activity was not restricted to one particular church. It embraced the whole church and, as a result, he was bound to use all the strength he had, to fulfill this duty perfectly and completely. In this way, he must give proof of his fidelity as a "steward of God's mysteries" (1 Cor. 4:1). It is demanded of such stewards that they should "prove themselves faithful" (1 Cor. 4:2).

[6]*My blood is already poured out as a drink-offering; the time has come for my return home.*

The dangerous situation in which the community found itself moved Paul to call upon Timothy to be utterly faithful and dedicated in the discharge of his duty. The position in which he personally found himself was an added motive. He writes to him with the thought of his approaching death firmly fixed in his mind. He knew that he had reached the end of his life, that he was inescapably doomed to die. He speaks of his death in two images. It was customary among pious Greeks or Romans who were pagans to offer drink-offerings in which part of the wine used was poured over the table, the hearth, or the altar, or into the sacrificial fire as an offering to the gods. The Jews, too, poured wine into the fire on the altar as a libation. In the same way, Paul's blood is now being poured out as an offering to God in his martyrdom; the sentence of death may fall any day. With these words, Paul asserts his conviction that his martyrdom is equivalent to a sacrifice in God's eyes (see Rev. 6:9). His suffering and death will benefit sinners, because " he endures everything for the sake of the elect " (2:10).

In a second image, he describes his death, which is imminent, as a *returning home to the Lord* in his Father's house (see Phil. 1:23). Both images underline Paul's willing and joyful acceptance of death. He realizes that it is by dying he will begin " to be with Christ " (Phil. 1:23); he is assured that he will " die in the Lord " (Rom. 14:8).

7 I have fought the good fight; I have finished the course; I have kept faith. 8 Now a crown of justice awaits me, which the Lord, just judge that he is, will give to me on that day, and not only to me, but to all those who have loved his coming.

Now that he has reached the end of his days, Paul looks back over the whole course of his life which he has completed. He has reached the goal. He can look back over his life with a clear conscience; he has fought an honorable *battle* in the service of the faith (see 1 Tim. 6:12). In all his labors, in all his sufferings and hardships, he had carefully preserved the whole basis and support of his life, his faith in Christ his Lord. Throughout his life, he was a real "servant of Christ and a steward of God's mysteries" (1 Cor. 4:1). He had lived up to the standard "set for all those who are stewards, namely, that they should prove themselves faithful" (1 Cor. 4:2). Like an athlete who has reached his goal, he can now look forward with certainty to the crown of victory. "On that day," the day of his glorious second coming, Christ, the just judge and glorified Lord, will give Paul the crown of victory, as a reward for a life which met with God's approval. This is the last of all the saving gifts Paul expects from the "just judge" (Gal. 5:5). However, he is also aware that he is not the only one who will receive this crown. That is why he adds that all those who have made use of their life on earth to prepare for the "coming" of the heavenly judge, and have learned to look forward to it with ardent love, will also receive the crown with him. This reminder is also intended to encourage and comfort his disciple.

Paul is filled with a strong faith and he faces death with a spirit which is unbowed and full of trust. For him, as for every Christian, death holds no more terrors; it is nothing more than a passing over, a return home to the Lord. Any Christian who, at the end of his days, can look back at a life which was spent in the service of his Lord like Paul's can expect the crown of victory from the hands of the just judge, just like him.

THE CLOSE OF THE LETTER
(4:9-22)

CONCLUSION (4:9–22)

Paul has come to the end of his letter properly so called. What follows is made up of news about his fellow workers (3:9–12) and a request directed to Timothy (4:13), together with a warning against Alexander the coppersmith (4:14–15). He then underlines once more the gravity of his position (4:16–18) and sends his last greetings (4:19–21). The letter concludes with a brief formula of good wishes (4:22) which has been accurately described as Paul's last will and testament.

News about Paul's Fellow Missionaries (4:9–12)

9*Hurry and come to me quickly!* 10*Demas has deserted me through love for this world and has gone to Thessalonica. Crescens has gone to Galatia and Titus to Dalmatia.* 11*Only Luke remains with me. Contact Mark and bring him with you: I can make good use of his services.* 12*I have sent Tychicus to Ephesus.*

Paul's life in prison at Rome was one of great loneliness. That is why he begs his beloved disciple to come to him; he was constantly in his thoughts, as he prayed for him and longed to see him (1:3–4). He must come as quickly as possible, before it is too late. Paul is afraid that, if he delays, he will never see him again in this world. In the loneliness of his detention, he had been bitterly disappointed in many of his friends. This is perhaps another reason why he calls upon Timothy so insistently. He has told us already that all the Christians from Asia had abandoned him, "among them Phigellus and Hermogenes" (1:15). He now explains what this meant: "At my first appearance in court no one stood by me. They all left me in the lurch" (4:16).

Demas was one of Paul's fellow workers and had accompanied him in his first imprisonment. He had allowed himself to be completely entangled by the affairs of this world and had deserted the Apostle in his captivity. His destination, Thessalonica, was a wealthy trading center. His desertion was probably the result of cowardice and reluctance to make sacrifices. He knew the dangers that his association with Paul involved and he scrambled to safety in good time. Crescens, about whom we know nothing further, probably went to "Galatia" in the service of the gospel. It seems clear that Galatia here means Gaul, not the province of Galatia in Asia Minor. It is very likely that Paul had preached the gospel in Spain a short time before. This makes it easier for us to understand why he should now send one of his fellow workers westwards once more.

Titus, who had left his post in Crete in the meantime and had returned to Paul in Rome (Tit. 3:12), had been given a new mission which took him to Dalmatia (see Rom. 15:19). Only Luke, the "beloved physician" (Col. 4:14), and Paul's faithful companion on his missionary journeys and in his first imprisonment, remained with him; he was still at his side. Another of his fellow workers was Mark. He had let Paul down on a previous occasion, but had afterwards completely corrected the bad impression he made. Together with Luke, he had remained steadfast at the Apostle's side in his first imprisonment, and now Paul needed his services. We can be sure this was for the work of the apostolate in Rome. He had sent him to Asia Minor (Col. 4:10) and now Timothy must bring him with him, when he comes to Rome.

Of Tychicus, who was another of Paul's assistants, we are told that he had been sent to Ephesus (Acts 20:4), his home town. There he could replace Timothy in his absence. He was a man whom Paul trusted implicitly. He had accompanied him on his voyage from Greece to Jerusalem (Acts 20:4) and had remained faithfully at his side during his first captivity. He had been commissioned by the Apostle to bring his letters to the communities of Ephesus and Colossae (Eph. 6:21f.; Col. 4:7f.). Now he must be deprived of his company, despite his loneliness.

The wonderfully human personality of the Apostle of the gentiles appears particularly clearly in these verses. Even now, on the very eve of his death, he was still intimately united with his fellow missionaries in fidelity and love. Their absence caused him pain and when they showed disloyalty he felt it keenly (4:10). Yet he sent them out to preach the good news. The gospel was spreading, despite his imprisonment; "God's word is not fettered" (2:9). His great love for Christ, his glorified Lord, had not diminished his love for his fellow laborers. On the contrary, it had enhanced and deepened it, raising it to a higher plane. At the end of his life, therefore, Paul stands before us as a great and high-minded man; he was a strong and well-rounded personality, and he maintained an intimate union with his fellow missionaries in faith and love until his death.

Paul Makes a Request of Timothy (4:13)

[13]*Bring with you the cloak I left with Carpus at Troas, when you come, and also the books, especially the parchments.*

Paul summons Timothy to him (4:9). On his way, he can bring

with him a number of things which Paul must have left at Troas on his last journey in the hands of a Christian named Carpus, who is otherwise unknown to us. His journey to Rome will take Timothy through Troas, after which he could take the Via Ignatia. Paul's request, therefore, will cause him no trouble. He will be able to bring him the cloak he left behind, a type of dress which in those days was worn only by the poorer sections of the population. It was a heavy garment used by travelers which covered the whole body. Paul could put it to good use in his cold prison during the winter which was approaching (4:21). Timothy must also bring Paul's "books" with him. These were undoubtedly papyrus rolls; and the "parchments," rolls of parchment which very likely contained the writings of the Old Testament. In the loneliness of his prison, Paul sought comfort and joy in his "books," in God's word in sacred scripture, as well as in the company of his faithful friends and fellow workers.

A Warning Against Alexander the Coppersmith

(4:14–15)

14*Alexander the coppersmith has caused me a lot of trouble. The Lord will repay as his actions deserve.* 15*You, too, must beware of him; he opposed our preaching strenuously.*

Two unhappy experiences from the past come to Paul's mind and he now mentions them to Timothy. A coppersmith named Alexander had caused him great sorrow by his bitter hostility and his passionate opposition to the preaching of the good news. We have no further information when or where this took place.

Neither is it clear whether this Alexander is the same person whom Paul had been compelled to hand over to Satan (1 Tim. 1:20). It is probable that he had taken a prominent part in the events which led to Paul's arrest; he may also have appeared as his prosecutor at Rome. Whatever the explanation, the wrong he inflicted on Paul must have been very great; the Apostle invokes *God's judgment* upon him in a phrase taken from the Old Testament. He is not influenced by his personal feelings or his irritation, much less by uncharitableness or enmity; he himself passes no judgment on him. He realizes that God is the proper judge in this situation; he will repay Alexander "as his actions deserve." He will have the last word at the final judgment. At the same time, Paul warns Timothy against him. He probably knew him from his activity in Ephesus.

The Gravity of Paul's Situation (4:16–18)

[16]*At my first defense no one stood by me; they all left me in*
the lurch. I pray that they will not be held to account for it.
[17]*Yet, God stood by me and gave me strength, so that the preach-*
ing of the gospel might reach its full achievement through me
and all nations might hear it. So I was snatched from the lion's
jaws. [18]*The Lord will rescue me from all evil and bring me to*
safety in his heavenly kingdom. To him belongs glory for all
ages. Amen.

Another unhappy memory comes to his mind, his first appearance in court at Rome which had already taken place. On that occasion, Paul had been bitterly disappointed: "They all left me in the lurch." These were the members of the Christian community at Rome who could have appeared as witnesses on his behalf, and his own fellow workers who had deserted him "out of love for this world" (4:10) and because they were afraid of the risk involved. In his hour of greatest danger, it had become frighteningly clear that none of his friends had the courage to stand by him. However, even in his greatest disappointment Paul shows himself a true disciple of his Lord, Jesus Christ, who forgave his enemies in the face of death (Lk. 23:34). Paul, too, can only pray for his unfaithful friends: "I pray that they will not be held to account for it."

His human friends had deserted Paul in his hour of trial, but not God. God had remained faithful to Jesus' promise: "When you are taken and given up like this, do not be worried beforehand what you should say. You must say whatever you are inspired to say at that moment. It is the Holy Spirit who will speak, not you" (Mk. 13:11; see Mt. 10:19–20). God himself had been his advocate, and his defense was successful. Even in his imprisonment Paul was so fired with zeal for his work as an apostle that he could think of the defense he must make in a matter of life and death only in terms of one thing; it gave him an opportunity of proclaiming the gospel. Even at this stage, his conduct was still inspired by the words he had once written to the church at Corinth: "I am under compulsion and it will be too bad for me, if I do not preach the gospel" (1 Cor. 9:16).

The defense that Paul made in court marked the end of his activity as an apostle. It gave him the opportunity to make known the good news before his pagan judges and before numerous witnesses from all parts of the world. So he fulfilled the divine commission entrusted to him literally to the very end of his life. When Paul was converted, our Lord told Ananias, "This man is my chosen instrument. He will make my name known before heathens and kings, and before the people of Israel. I will show him what he will have to suffer for my name's sake" (Acts 9:15f.).

By God's help he had once again been rescued from the "lion's jaws," from imminent peril to his life. But Paul knew only too well that his escape from the death sentence only postponed what was inevitable. He expected his case to come up again and he had no doubts about the outcome. He no longer hoped for acquittal. On the other hand, he was convinced that an even greater salvation awaited him, something far more glorious than merely escaping execution. God will deliver him and rescue him from "all evil"; he will save him from all earthly perils and bring him into his heavenly kingdom. His death as a martyr will open to him the doors of God's kingdom and his ardent wish will be fulfilled. He had once written to the church at Philippi: "I long to be quit of it all and to be with Christ. That is by far the better thing" (Phil. 1:23). The mention of God's power and grace moves Paul to praise him, as was customary with pious Jews. The readers were meant to make this prayer their own by joining in the "Amen."

In these verses, as in 3:6–8, Paul's gaze is fixed unwaveringly on the death which awaited him. Inspired by deep faith as he was, and fully conscious of his intimate union with his glorified Lord, Jesus Christ, he regarded death merely as a way of entering into eternal joy; it gave him access to that glory which abides with the Father.

Greetings (4:19–21)

19 *Greet Prisca and Aquila and the household of Onesiphorus.*
20 *Erastus remained at Corinth and Trophimus was ill, so I left*

him at Miletus. [21]*Hurry and come before it is winter. Eubulus, Pudens, Linus, Claudia, and all the brothers send you their greetings.*

As in nearly all of Paul's letters, a list of greetings now follows. These are sent in the first place to Prisca and Aquila, his faithful collaborators in all his missionary activities. They had once saved him from death at the risk of their own lives (Rom. 16:3f.). As in a previous passage (1:16–18), Paul also mentions the "household," that is, the family of Onesiphorus who had proved so faithful. We can be sure he himself was already dead. It is not clear whether Timothy and those who are mentioned with him were still in Ephesus at the time Paul was writing this letter (see 4:12). As a postscript to the information he has already given us (4:9–12), he now mentions two more details about his fellow workers. Erastus, who is probably the city treasurer from Corinth mentioned in Romans 16:23, had remained behind in his native city. Paul had once sent him with Timothy from Ephesus into Macedonia (Acts 19:22). Trophimus, who came from Ephesus (Acts 21:29), was another collaborator of Paul's. He had accompanied him on his voyage from Greece to Jerusalem (Acts 20:4). In his last journey before his imprisonment, which must have taken him through Troas (4:13) to Miletus, Paul had been forced to leave his faithful companion behind there, because he was ill.

Paul now begs Timothy for the second time to come to him without delay (see 4:9). He must hurry as winter is approaching and travel by sea will be impossible. The death sentence may come at any moment. That is why he appeals to him so insistently once again to make a quick start; otherwise his disciple may never see his master alive again.

These verses conclude with greetings from the Christian community at Rome where Paul was imprisoned. Four are mentioned by name; these were undoubtedly known to Timothy. Of these, Linus is quite possibly identical with the person of the same name who was later bishop of Rome and the first successor of the apostle Peter. Of the others we know nothing definite.

Good Wishes (4:22)

22*May the Lord be with your spirit! Grace be with all of you.*

Paul concludes his letter with a blessing for his beloved disciple, Timothy, and for the whole church in which he was active, which never left Paul's thoughts. The Apostle of the gentiles sends him the greatest wish any Christian can send another, "grace," God's favor by which we are saved (Eph. 2:5, 8). At the moment it is still invisible, but it will eventually be revealed in all its glory in the "world to come" (Eph. 2:7).